# The Nature of Intention

The Nature of emotion

# The Nature of Intention

*Jack W. Meiland*

Methuen & Co Ltd . London

First published 1970
by Methuen & Co. Ltd
11 New Fetter Lane, London EC4
© 1970 Jack W. Meiland
Printed in Great Britain by
Richard Clay (The Chaucer Press) Ltd
Bungay, Suffolk

416 14690 2

To Rosalie

Distributed in the U.S.A.
by Barnes & Noble Inc.

# Contents

v

# Acknowledgements

I wish to thank William P. Alston, Vere C. Chappell, Arnold Kaufman, Fred A. Siegler, James O. Urmson, and my students in Philosophy 609 at the University of Michigan for their helpful comments on parts or all of an earlier draft of this book. Roy F. Holland made numerous comments on the whole manuscript and gave other assistance far beyond the call of duty. The comments of David Pears resulted in important improvements in several chapters. The final draft has also benefited from the suggestions of the editor, Patrick Taylor.

I also wish to thank the Executive Board of the Horace H. Rackham School of Graduate Studies of the University of Michigan for the award of a Faculty Research Fellowship for the Spring–Summer Term of 1965. The Rackham School also provided funds for the typing of the final draft. Mrs Alice Gantt did the typing of the several drafts with her usual accuracy and dispatch.

# Introduction

My purpose in this book is to delineate some of the important characteristics of intentions and thereby to take a first step towards a satisfactory theory of intention. In this introduction I wish to explain why a satisfactory theory of intention is desirable, both in order to demonstrate the importance of this topic and in order to show more clearly what sorts of matters I will discuss in this book. The philosophical importance of a satisfactory theory of intention may be conveniently discussed under three headings: (i) the philosophy of mind, (ii) the problem of free will, (iii) ethical and legal contexts.

Intentions and purposes are not the only sorts of mental entities or states that are attributed to persons by themselves or others. Confining our attention to those entities and states loosely classified under 'the will', we find desires, likings, cravings, aversions, and deliberations, in addition to intentions and purposes. We say such things as 'Baxter wants to visit his brother-in-law' as well as 'Baxter intends to visit his brother-in-law'. But it is clear that intentions and purposes play a pervasive role in our mental lives and that many, if not most, of the things that we do are done with certain intentions or for certain purposes. Consequently, no theory of the mind can be adequate unless it provides a satisfactory account of intention. Some of the questions which arise in this area concern the characteristics of intentions by themselves without any particular relation to other mental states or events. Are intentions 'inner events' or occurrences, or are they instead dispositions of a fairly complex sort? Are they publicly knowable, or are they a sort of thing about which only the agent can know with certainty? If they are publicly knowable, what are the criteria (if any) for attributing intentions to others? Do these criteria show that animals can have intentions and purposes? Do these criteria allow the possibility of unconscious intentions? Even apart from such criteria, does it make sense to talk about unconscious intentions and purposes? What sorts of things can be intended? Are there different types of intentions?

A second group of questions concerns the relations between intentions and other mental states and activities. Is deciding to perform some action $X$ identical with intending to perform $X$, or does some other relation exist between these? How is the intention to do $X$ related to deliberating about doing $X$, choosing to do $X$, and trying to do $X$? Are there any beliefs which the agent must have in order to intend to do $X$? I think that these questions make it clear that a satisfactory theory of intention would map out a large part of the sphere of the mental and would thus form an essential element of a theory of the mind.

Of equal importance is the bearing of the topic of intention of the problem of free will. Intentions have sometimes been regarded as causing actions. And it has seemed to some philosophers that if intentions themselves were the effects of factors outside the agent's control – genetic endowment, upbringing, present environment, etc. – then those actions caused by intentions would themselves ultimately be caused by these factors too, hence not under the agent's control, and hence not be free. If all of this were so, it would powerfully reinforce the view that man is simply a part of nature, subject to natural laws in the same way as anything else in the world, and therefore not a unique being standing outside the order of nature as has sometimes been claimed. On the other hand, some have claimed that not only are intentions not the causes of actions but also that intentions logically cannot be causes of actions even though they 'issue' in actions. This would, perhaps, provide some support for the view that man stands outside the order of nature. This topic is often discussed under the heading of 'the explanation of action', with the question being put in a somewhat different way: are explanations of actions in terms of intentions and purposes causal explanations?

Positions on the problem of free will have often been claimed to have implications for the ethical and legal assessment of actions. Some believe that if actions are not free, then it does not make sense to hold the agent responsible for them or to praise, blame, reward, or punish him for what he does. But intention comes into this matter in a more direct way too. For some philosophers have held that a person is responsible only for those actions done 'with intention' or only for those actions which he intentionally performed. Obviously such claims as these raise many important questions. What is it for an action to be intentional? Is every intentional action one which the person intended to perform? What is the difference between an action's being intentional and its being voluntary? There is also a quite different way in which intention may be involved in the ethical assessment of actions, namely with respect to the relation between the value of the intention and the value of the action. For example, Abelard held that an action is good not because it 'contains within it some good' but instead because it 'issues from a good intention'. In the legal sphere, the main concern has been with identifying the notion of intention used in the law and with criticizing that notion. For example, it has been claimed that the legal notion of intention differs significantly from the notion of intention employed in everyday life and, moreover, that the law would be more just if it employed the ordinary notion of intention instead.

This brief outline should serve to show that the topic of intention is quite broad and includes many different kinds of questions. In this book I am concerned almost entirely with questions belonging to the first area, the philosophy of mind. The philosophy of mind is important in its own right. For an adequate theory of mind will help us know better what man is. Moreover, it seems to me that answers to some of the questions in the other areas may depend to some extent on answers to questions in the philosophy of mind. For example, if it turns out that intentions are dispositions, it may be more difficult to see how intentions can be causes of actions. For it may not be clear how a disposition can be a cause of anything.

There is a sense of the expression 'telling what a thing is' in which to tell what something is is to tell what its characteristics are. In this sense of that expression, I try in this book to tell what intentions are. It is for this reason that I have called this book *The Nature of Intention*. To this end, I describe certain facts and propose and defend certain theses about intentions. There is, perhaps, another sense of the expression 'telling what a thing is' in which to tell what a thing is is to do something over and above telling what its characteristics are. For example, in the case of intentions, this might involve placing intentions within an exhaustive classification of mental entities, describing the similarities and differences between intentions and other types of mental entities, and so on. This is done to some extent here, particularly in Part Two. This might also involve giving a general theory of intention which holds that an intention is something of a certain general sort, such as a belief or a disposition, and which thereby tries to account for all of the various characteristics of intentions. Although I do not

3

put forth any such theory here, some theories of this sort are discussed in Part Three. In any case what I try to do in this book is a necessary prolegomenon to an adequate general theory of intention. For a given general theory of intention will be adequate only if it accounts for all of the characteristics of intentions. And we can determine whether or not a given general theory of intention is adequate only if we know what the characteristics of intentions are. Determining what some of the major characteristics of intentions are is the main purpose of this book.

The overall plan of the book is this. In Part One I distinguish and discuss several different types of intentions. Chapter 3 concerns the types of things that intentions can be about. Part Two deals mainly with the relations between intentions and other sorts of mental states or entities. And Part Three consists of a discussion of several general theories of intention.

PART ONE

# Types and Objects of Intention

# 1 Purposive intentions and non-purposive intentions

## 1. *Introduction*

In this chapter, I wish to show that there are two very different types of intentions and what some of the differences between these two types of intentions are. I call intentions of the first type 'non-purposive intentions' (or, more briefly, 'intentions$_1$'); and I call intentions of the second type 'purposive intentions' (or 'intentions$_2$').

## 2. *Examples of Each of the Two Types*

Suppose that Jones intends to drive his car downtown and believes that his doing so will cause wear on the engine's crankshaft. Does he therefore also intend to cause wear on that crankshaft? It would probably seem incorrect to many people to say that this person intends to cause wear on that part. I believe that this is not incorrect, however. This *seems* incorrect because it *is* incorrect to say that it was his intention in driving downtown to cause wear on the crankshaft. And the term 'intends' is often and perhaps even usually used in this way to talk about what might be called 'the agent's intention *in* performing a certain action'.

But there are other uses of 'intends'. To take another case, suppose that there is civil strife in the South American republic of Paraduras and that Señor Espinoza, the respected elder statesman, has been asked by the contending factions to do whatever will bring peace to the country. Espinoza decides that the first step is to appoint as president a man acceptable to both sides. He knows that there is only one such man – Garcia, a fifty-year-old former cabinet minister. And one of the things that Espinoza believes about Garcia is that the latter is fifty years old. Espinoza decides to appoint Garcia to the presidency. So the statement 'Espinoza intends to appoint Garcia to the presidency' is true. But, it seems to me, the statement 'Espinoza intends to appoint

7

a fifty-year-old man to the presidency' is also true. Espinoza intends to appoint Garcia, and believes that to appoint Garcia is to appoint a fifty-year-old man; and because of this, he intends to appoint a fifty-year-old man.

Now let us suppose that in order to appoint a new president Espinoza must convoke the National Assembly of Paraduras, for a new president can be appointed in these circumstances only with the consent of the National Assembly. And let us also suppose that someone asks Espinoza why he is convoking the National Assembly. To explain this, Espinoza can truly say, 'It is my intention to appoint Garcia to the presidency.' But it would be, at the very least, misleading for him to say, 'It is my intention to appoint a fifty-year-old man to the presidency.' The first statement would be true and the second at least misleading because the expression 'It is my intention to . . .' is used to express the agent's *purpose*. For an agent to say, 'It is my intention to do $X$', when asked why he is doing or intends to do $Y$ is for that agent to say, 'The *intention with which* I am doing $Y$ is to do $X$' or '*My intention in doing $Y$ is to do $X$*' or '*My purpose in doing $Y$ is to do $X$*'. And it is certainly not Espinoza's purpose to appoint a fifty-year-old man to the presidency. If Garcia were instead forty-nine years old, Espinoza would still appoint him.

Thus, the reason why it seems incorrect, though it is in fact *not* incorrect, to say in the first case we considered that Jones intends to cause wear on his engine's crankshaft is perhaps that it is believed that saying 'He intends to . . .' is synonymous with saying 'It is his intention to . . .'. But these are not synonymous. For an agent can intend to do $X$ without the doing of $X$ being his intention *in* doing something else or his *purpose* in doing something else, as Espinoza's appointing a fifty-year-old man is not his purpose in doing what he is doing when he convokes the National Assembly.

This second case involves two intentions: the intention to appoint a fifty-year-old man to the presidency and the intention to appoint Garcia to the presidency.[1] These two intentions are examples of the two types of intentions which I am distinguishing from one another and discussing in this chapter. I will use the terms 'non-purposive intentions' and 'intentions$_1$' to refer to the class of intentions to which the intention to appoint a fifty-year-old man to the presidency belongs And I will use the terms 'purposive intentions' and 'intentions$_2$' to

[1] Here I am using the principle 'different descriptions, different intentions'.

refer to the class of intentions to which the intention to appoint Garcia to the presidency belongs. I call the second class 'the class of purposive intentions' because Espinoza's intention to appoint Garcia to the presidency is the intention *with which* he does something else (for example, convokes the National Assembly) or his *purpose* in doing something else. His intention to appoint a fifty-year-old man to the presidency is not his purpose in doing anything else, and so I call the class to which this intention belongs 'the class of non-purposive intentions'. However, I do not wish to say that the class of purposive intentions consists of all and only intentions which are 'intentions with which' or purposes. An intention's being or not being an intention with which the agent does or will do something else is not the criterion of that intention's belonging to the class of purposive intentions. Some of the criteria of which class of intentions a given intention belongs are described in the next section. If an intention satisfies these criteria (perhaps among others), then that intention is a purposive intention even if that intention is not an intention with which the agent does or will do something else. As we will see in Section 4, not all intentions which are very similar in these ways to 'intentions with which' and which thus belong to the class of purposive intentions are themselves 'intentions with which'. The class of purposive intentions or intentions$_2$ includes intentions which are not 'intentions with which'. We may use the term 'intentions$_2$' as a neutral name for this class. But in describing the differences between the two classes of intention in question I will use 'intentions with which' as the prime examples of intentions$_2$.

## 3. *Some Differences between non-purposive Intentions and Purposive Intentions*

Let us suppose that John's prospective purpose in doing $Z$ is to bring it about that $K$ and that John knows that one cannot bring it about that $K$ without bringing it about that $L$. However, bringing it about that $L$ is not one of John's purposes in doing $Z$. Yet, if what I have claimed in Section 2 is true, John does intend to bring it about that $L$. For John intends to bring it about that $K$ since bringing it about that $K$ is the intention with which he is doing or will do $Z$. And since John intends to bring it about that $K$ and John believes that bringing it about that $K$ is inseparable from bringing it about that $L$, John intends to bring it about that $L$.[1] (Of course, this latter intending is intending$_1$.)

Now we can describe some differences between intending$_1$ and intending$_2$. The first difference concerns trying. Although John (in the case just described) intends to bring it about that $L$, when John does $Z$, we would not describe John as trying to bring it about that $L$. We would instead describe him as trying to bring it about that $K$. There seems to be no situation in which we would describe an agent as trying to do something that he intended to do (say, $X$) where the intention to do $X$ is like John's intention to bring it about that $L$. An intention that is an intention$_1$ is not an intention which the agent can try to carry out. But the agent can try to carry out an in-

[1] It might be said that the reason why bringing it about that $K$ is the intention with which John does $Z$ and bringing it about that $L$ is not an 'intention with which', even though both $K$ and $L$ are expected by John as results of his doing $Z$, is that the agent desires that $K$ be the case and does not desire that $L$ be the case (nor does he believe that, for example, it is his duty to bring it about that $L$ or have some other sort of motive directed at bringing it about that $L$). But this seems to be incorrect. The agent can desire that $L$ be the case and yet do $Z$ for the purpose of bringing it about that $K$. That $L$ comes to be the case is perhaps an additional benefit which John derives from performing $Z$, but it is not necessarily therefore his purpose in performing $Z$. It may then be replied that this is possible only if to say that bringing it about that $L$ is not his purpose in doing $Z$ and bringing it about that $K$ is his purpose in doing $Z$ is to say that if doing $Z$ were believed by the agent not to result in $L$ but were still believed to result in $K$, the agent would still do $Z$, whereas if he believed that $K$ would not result but $L$ would result, he would not do $Z$. But this is also incorrect. If the agent does desire that $L$ be the case, then he might do $Z$ if he believes that doing $Z$ will not bring it about that $K$ but will bring it about that $L$. That doing $Z$ brings it about that $L$ is not *now* his reason for doing $Z$. But if he comes to believe that doing $Z$ will not bring it about that $K$, then he may come to have as his reason for doing $Z$ that doing $Z$ brings it about that $L$. But in the kind of case which we are now discussing, this is not his reason for doing $Z$ while he believes that doing $Z$ brings it about that $K$. Thus, it is not true that if 'bringing it about that $L$' is not the intention with which the agent does $Z$ even though he expects $L$ to thereby be brought about, then the agent would not do $Z$ if he believed that doing $Z$ brought it about solely that $L$. Again, it is not the case that if 'bringing it about that $K$' is the agent's intention in doing $Z$, then if the agent came to believe that doing $Z$ did not in fact bring it about that $K$, he would not do $Z$. For he might then do $Z$ because he believes that doing $Z$ brings it about that $L$. (It should be noted that the kind of case being discussed here is different from the kind in which the agent from the beginning has two purposes in doing $Z$, neither of which is sufficient alone but which are jointly sufficient.)

tention which is an intention$_2$, such as John's intention to bring it about that $K$.

The second difference to be brought out here is this. In the above situation, John can change his mind about bringing it about that $K$. He can decide not to bring it about that $K$. But he cannot decide not to bring it about that $L$. John cannot change his mind about bringing it about that $L$ in the above case. When he does what might be regarded as deciding not to bring it about that $L$, what he does would instead be described in another way. It would be described as follows: 'He decided not to bring it about that $K$ because he believed that bringing it about that $K$ was inseparable, at least in that situation, from bringing it about that $L$ and he did not want to bring it about that $L$.' That is, we would refer to his attitude towards 'bringing it about that $L$' as a *desire* not to bring it about that $L$ and would cite this desire as an explanation of why he changed his mind *about bringing it about that $K$*. It is 'bringing it about that $K$' about which he changes his mind in this case, not 'bringing it about that $L$'.

Thus, there are at least two conditions – pertaining to trying and to the agent's changing his mind – which an intention has to satisfy in order to be what I have called a purposive intention or an intention$_2$. Moreover, any intention which does satisfy these conditions is an intention$_2$. These conditions are each necessary conditions of an intention's being an intention$_2$. Thus, for example, if an intention is not one which the agent can try to carry out or about which he can change his mind, that intention does not belong to the class of purposive intentions as I am using the expression 'purposive intention'. And these two conditions are together sufficient for an intention's being an intention$_2$ or a purposive intention.

An intention that is an intention$_1$ is thus very different from an intention that is an intention$_2$. In later chapters we will be talking almost exclusively about intentions$_2$. It is intentions of this sort – intentions that, for example, the agent can try to carry out – that are most often attributed to agents. There is, as we have seen, another sense of 'intention' (that expressed by 'intention$_1$') which expresses a relation between the agent and a possible future action since such statements as 'Espinoza intends to appoint a fifty-year-old man to the presidency' are true. But these two senses of 'intention' are very different from one another, as I have tried to show. And it is primarily with intentions$_2$ that we will be concerned.

### 4. *Means and Intending*$_2$

Thus far, the only examples of purposive intentions or intentions$_2$ that I have given have been 'intentions with which' – 'intentions *with which* the agent does something or which are the agent's intentions *in doing* something. Consider now the following type of situation. The agent intends to bring it about that $K$ and decides to perform action $Y$ in order to bring it about that $K$. Hence, 'bringing it about that K' is the agent's intention in doing $Y$ and thus is intended$_2$. It is possible that the agent's intention to perform $Y$ is *not* an intention with which he performs or will perform still another action. If the agent's intention to perform $Y$ is not the intention with which he performs or will perform some other action, then the agent's intention to perform $Y$ is not itself an 'intention with which'. Is, then, the agent's intention to do $Y$ a purposive intention or an intention$_2$ even when that intention to do $Y$ is not his purpose in doing something else?

It seems clear that even in this situation the agent's intention to do $Y$ is an intention$_2$. The agent here intends to perform $Y$ as a means to bringing it about that $K$. And an intention to perform a certain action as a means is an intention which the agent can try to carry out. Second, an intention to perform an action as a means is an intention which the agent can cease to have as a result of changing his mind about performing that action. He may, for example, decide to use some other means. Thus, an intention to perform a certain action as a means is an intention$_2$.

There is even some warrant for applying the term 'purposive' to intentions to perform actions as means. It is true that there is a great difference between something's being the agent's purpose *in* his doing something else and his doing something *for* a certain purpose. And it is true that if the agent intends to do $Y$ as a means, $Y$ may not be the agent's purpose *in* doing something else. But the agent still intends to do $Y$ *for* a certain *purpose*. Means and ends are linked together by purposes. And this provides some justification for continuing to call intentions$_2$ 'purposive intentions' even though intentions to do actions as means are intentions$_2$ and yet are not 'intentions with which' or purposes.

There may be intentions which are not associated with purposes in any way at all and yet meet the two conditions of being intentions$_2$. Such intentions would then be intentions$_2$ regardless of their lack of association with purposes.

## 5. *Inseparability of Intentions*

Let us say that an *action X* is *inseparable* from another action *Y* if and only if to perform *X* is to perform *Y*, or if and only if one cannot perform *X* without also (perhaps in the course of performing *X*) performing *Y*. Otherwise let us say that *X* is *separable* from *Y*. As an example of these relations, an agent cannot run without moving his feet, but he can move his feet without running; therefore, running is inseparable from moving one's feet, but the latter is separable from the former. In a similar way, the *intention* to do *X* may be said to be inseparable from the *intention* to do *Y* if and only if it is the case that if the agent intends to do *X*, he also intends to do *Y*. Otherwise, the first intention will be said to be separable from the second intention.

Let us now apply these notions of separability and inseparability of intentions to the examples given earlier in this chapter. If we were to apply these notions in, so to speak, their pure and unrestricted form, we would be concerned with the following questions: (i) If Jones intends to drive his car downtown and if to do so involves causing wear on the crankshaft, does Jones intend to cause wear on the crankshaft (regardless of his beliefs or lack of beliefs about the wear on the crankshaft); (ii) if Espinoza intends to appoint Garcia and Garcia is fifty years old, does Espinoza intend to appoint a fifty-year-old man (regardless of Espinoza's beliefs about Garcia's age)? The question here is: is one intention inseparable from another, given a certain fact about the world? In the first case, the fact in question is that driving the car will cause wear on the crankshaft. In the second case, the fact is that Garcia is fifty years old. It may seem *prima facie* that the intentions are separable in these cases. On the other hand, if to have the intention to do *X* is also to have the intention to do whatever is involved in doing *X*, then these intentions may be inseparable (given the above-mentioned facts about the world).

However this may be, there is inseparability of these intentions provided that the agent has certain beliefs. In the first case, if Jones intends to drive downtown and *believes* that to do so will cause wear on the crankshaft, then he intends to cause wear on the crankshaft. And if Espinoza intends to appoint Garcia and *believes* that Garcia is fifty years old, then he intends to appoint a fifty-year-old man. This may be regarded as a restricted form of inseparability of intentions: the restriction or condition is that the agent has certain beliefs.

One important feature of the inseparability of intentions is that the relation of inseparability can hold both within and across the categories of purposive and non-purposive intentions. This is to say that if the intention to do $X$ is inseparable from the intention to do $Y$ in the restricted way just described, then these two intentions may be of the same type or of different types. To put this in another way, if the intention to do $X$ is inseparable from the intention to do $Y$, and we know that the intention to do $X$ is a purposive intention, nothing follows from this about the category to which the intention to do $Y$ belongs. The Espinoza–Garcia case provides an example of a purposive intention (the intention to appoint Garcia) which is inseparable from a non-purposive intention (the intention to appoint a fifty-year-old man). But the relation can hold within one of these categories too. For example, an agent might perform some action which has two purposes. Thus, he has two purposive intentions. And these intentions might stand in the relation of inseparability. A man might walk to the stationery store to buy some stationery because he wishes to send a letter to a friend. He has two purposive intentions – to buy stationery and to write a letter to his friend. Now if we suppose that the agent believes that he can write a letter to his friend only if he buys stationery at the store, then his intention to write a letter to his friend is inseparable from his intention to buy stationery at the store. And since these are both purposive intentions in this case, here we have two purposive intentions which stand in the relation of inseparability.

So purposive and non-purposive intentions do not seem to differ as to their ability to stand in the relation of inseparability. Nor do they seem to differ with respect to the kinds of intentions to which they can stand in this relation. But, judging from the cases we have discussed in this chapter, the following is a reasonable hypothesis as to one way in which these two kinds of intentions might exhibit disparate properties with respect to inseparability: If a purposive intention is inseparable from a non-purposive intention, then the agent has the non-purposive intention solely because he has the purposive intention; but if a purposive intention is inseparable from another purposive intention, while it may be the case that the agent must have the latter intention in virtue of having the former, it is not the case that the latter intention is one of his *purposes* solely because he has the former intention. A decision about the truth or falsity of this hypothesis must await a fuller description of the members of the classes of purposive and non-purposive intentions.

# 2 Non-conditional intentions and conditional intentions

## 1. Introduction

An agent may intend to do *X* if *C* obtains. For example, an agent may intend to go downtown tomorrow if it doesn't rain. Or he may intend to go to New York on Wednesday if Jones is there. In the first case, the agent intends the following: to go downtown tomorrow if it doesn't rain. In the second case, the agent intends the following: to go to New York on Wednesday if Jones is there. In each case, the condition – 'If it doesn't rain' or 'If Jones is there' – is not a condition of the agent's intending to go downtown tomorrow or his intending to go to New York. That is, these conditions are not conditions of his having these intentions. Instead, these conditions are part of what the agent intends.[1]

When an agent intends *to do an action X if circumstances C are present*, his performance of *X* is subject to a condition *as part of what he intends*. If, instead, he could *completely* express his intention by saying 'I intend to do *X*' when asked what he intends to do, his doing of *X*, *in so far as what he intends is concerned*, does not depend upon the fulfilment of a condition (although, as we will see, his doing of *X* may be subject to a condition in another way). Intentions of the first sort (examples of which were given in the previous paragraph) will be called 'conditional intentions', while those of the second sort will be called 'unconditional intentions'.

The thesis that conditional intentions and unconditional intentions are different types of intentions – and what the fundamental difference between them is – can be put in terms of the notion of an object of an intention. In this chapter and in the rest of this book (particularly in Chapter 3), I will use the expression 'object of an intention' in the

---

[1] A conditional intention might be represented thus: Smith intends (to go to New York on Wednesday if Jones is there).

following way: the object of an intention is what is intended. The object is what the intention is about. Thus, the intention to go to New York and the intention to go to Chicago have different objects. One is about the action 'going to New York' and the other is about the action 'going to Chicago'. If an intention has $X$ as its object, I will sometimes say that that intention is 'directed at $X$'. Now the fundamental difference between conditional intentions pertaining to actions and unconditional intentions pertaining to actions can be put in the following way. These two types of intentions have different types of objects: unconditional intentions have *actions* as their objects; conditional intentions have *actions performed in certain circumstances* as their objects.

In Sections 2 and 6 it is shown that unconditional and conditional intentions are in fact different types of intentions. That they have these very different properties is due to the fact that conditional intentions and unconditional intentions have different types of objects. In Sections 3 and 4, it is shown that conditional intentions cannot be construed as or reduced to unconditional intentions. Furthermore, what is said in Section 6 shows that unconditional intentions cannot be construed as sets of conditional intentions. Hence, these types of intentions are distinct from one another. In Section 5 a type of intention called 'temporally conditional intentions' – those having objects of the type 'to do $X$ at $t_i$', that is, in the complete expression of which a time-specification and no other condition is included – is shown to be similar in some respects to both conditional and unconditional intentions and to be a third separate and distinct type of intention. Both unconditional intentions and temporally conditional intentions will be said to be 'non-conditional', since they do not involve circumstances of the sort involved in conditional intentions.

Thus, I wish to show that these are in fact different types of intentions and in what respects they are different. I will also make a suggestion about why they differ in these ways.

## 2. *The Conditional Object Position*

A statement of a conditional intention has the form 'He intends to do $X$ if $C$ obtains', where '$C$' stands for circumstances which may be present in some future situation. Thus the object of a conditional intention is not merely '$X$' but instead '$X$ if $C$ obtains'. The object of the

16

intention contains a condition; the condition is in some way *part of what is intended or part of what the intention is about*. Let us call this position – that the condition is in some way part of what is intended – the 'Conditional Object' position. This is the view which I wish to maintain in this chapter. On this view, actions by themselves are not the only objects of intentions. For conditional objects – that is, actions together with circumstances – can be objects of intentions too.

That there are conditional intentions and that they are different from unconditional intentions can be seen in the following way. An agent can intend to do $X$ at $t_i$ if $C$ obtains at $t_i$ and at the same time correctly believe that $C$ will not obtain at $t_i$. So in this sort of case the agent's subsequently coming to know prior to $t_i$ that $C$ will not obtain at $t_i$ cannot lead him to change his mind about that which he intended to do. He will perhaps not do $X$ at $t_i$, but not because he changed his mind about doing $X$ at $t_i$. Instead, he will not do $X$ at $t_i$ because $C$ will not be present at $t_i$. This is very different from the case of an unconditional intention. If the agent intends to do $X$ at $t_i$ and then finds that $C$, which he had expected to be present at $t_i$, will not in fact be present at $t_i$, he may change his mind about doing $X$ at $t_i$. He may decide not to do $X$ at $t_i$ because $C$ will not be present at $t_i$. But an agent who intends *to do $X$ at $t_i$ if $C$ obtains at $t_i$* cannot change his mind about doing $X$ at $t_i$ *on the grounds that $C$ will not then be present*. And this is so even if it is the case that if $C$ will not be present at $t_i$ he will in fact not do $X$ at $t_i$ because $C$ will not in fact be present at $t_i$.

A second difference between unconditional and conditional intentions which is closely related to the one just discussed is this. If one of the agent's reasons for *having the unconditional intention of doing $X$ at $t_i$* is that he believes that $C$ will be present at $t_i$, then if $C$ is present at $t_i$ and the agent believes this, that $C$ is present is *also* one of his reasons for doing $X$ at $t_i$ (unless the agent has changed his mind about the presence of $C$ or about doing $X$ at all in the meantime). But if his intention is a conditional intention, this is not necessarily so. If his intention is conditional, the following can be true: (1) the presence of $C$ at $t_i$ is a reason for the agent's *doing $X$ at $t_i$*; and yet (2) a belief that $C$ will be present at $t_i$ is *not* a reason for his having the intention of doing $X$ at $t_i$. For an agent can have the conditional intention 'to do $X$ at $t_i$ if $C$ obtains' and yet believe that $C$ will not obtain at $t_i$. The two cases may differ, then, in whether the belief that $C$ will be present at $t_i$ is a reason for having the intention.

A third difference is this. Unless he changes his mind about doing $X$, comes to believe that it is not possible for him to do $X$, or is prevented from trying to do $X$, the agent cannot have an *unconditional* intention to do $X$ and at the same time not have the belief that he will try to do $X$. (The unconditional intention is, however, not identical with this belief, as we will see in Chapter 9). But the agent who has the *conditional* intention to do $X$ if $C$ is present can at the same time not believe that he will try to do $X$ unless he changes his mind about doing $X$, comes to believe that it is not possible for him to do $X$, or is prevented from trying to do $X$. For he can have this conditional intention while believing that $C$ will never be present. And on these grounds he may believe that he will not try to do $X$ even though he will not change his mind about doing $X$, will not come to believe that it is not possible for him to do X, and will be not prevented from trying to do $X$.

The differences just stated have been said to be differences between conditional intentions and unconditional intentions. I have talked as if the agent's intention with respect to $X$ is either conditional or unconditional and cannot be both conditional and unconditional. However, the agent's intention with respect to $X$ can be both conditional and unconditional. *For his intention to do $X$ can be conditional with respect to one circumstance $C_1$ and unconditional with respect to another circumstance $C_2$ at one and the same time.* What it is for an intention to be conditional with respect to $C_1$ and unconditional with respect to $C_2$ is partly for the three differences described above to be differences between this one intention in its relation to $C_1$, on the one hand, and this one intention in its relation to $C_2$ on the other. So while I have put these three differences as differences between types of intentions, they should in fact be construed as differences between conditionality of intention and unconditionality of intention. The description of these differences constitutes at least a partial description of the difference between conditionality and unconditionality. And conditionality and unconditionality can occur, so to speak, within a single intention, as well as be a difference between two different intentions.

It might be said that every intention is conditional with respect to at least some conditions even if no condition is expressed when the intention is expressed. For it is taken for granted that the action in question will be performed if or only if certain conditions obtain. For example, if an agent says, 'I intend to drive downtown tomorrow,' his intention is expressed in just the way in which an unconditional intention is expressed. So it appears to be an unconditional intention. But it is understood that he will not drive downtown tomorrow if a severe snowstorm makes the roads impassable. His intention is in fact conditional with respect to the possibility of a snowstorm. But the agent does not mention this condition because this condition is taken for granted. There is no need to mention this condition since everyone knows that this is a condition of his driving downtown tomorrow.

Perhaps it is true that every intention is, as a matter of fact, conditional with respect to at least one circumstance. My theory of conditionality can allow this. For I do *not* claim that the criterion of whether or not an intention is conditional with respect to a given circumstance is whether the agent *mentions* that circumstance in expressing his intention. An agent can express *an intention* which is in fact conditional with respect to some circumstance without expressing *its conditionality* by mentioning that circumstance. Some of the criteria of whether or not an intention is conditional with respect to a given circumstance have already been given in describing the three differences between conditionality and unconditionality.[1] For example, a given circumstance $C_1$ *is* a circumstance with respect to which the agent's intention to do $X$ is conditional only if the agent's coming to believe that $C_1$ will not occur cannot serve as a reason for his changing his mind about doing $X$. The agent *mentions* the conditions on which his doing of $X$ is conditional when he believes that the hearer does not know that his doing of $X$ is conditional on these conditions or when he wishes, for one reason or another, to stress these conditions of his doing $X$.

Nevertheless, there is an important difference between two sorts of circumstances which the agent does *not* mention in expressing his intention. These two groups of circumstances are: (i) circumstances which satisfy the criteria mentioned in the description of the three differences above and with respect to which the agent's intention is conditional; (ii) circumstances which satisfy the criteria mentioned in the description of the three differences above and with respect to which the agent's intention is not conditional. This is to say that a circumstance's satisfying the criteria mentioned above is not sufficient for the agent's intention to be conditional with respect to that circumstance. For there can be a circumstance which satisfies these three criteria and yet the agent does not know or believe that this circumstance is a condition of his performing the action. Let us suppose that

[1] Another criterion will be given in Section 6.

the agent would not change his mind about doing $X$ if he learned that $C$ would not occur, and yet that the agent does not realize that this is so. Then he does not intend to do $X$ if $C$ occurs. $C$ is no part of what he intends. $C$ does not enter into his intention at all, although $C$ might become part of his intention if he realized that $C$ was relevant to the doing of $X$ or to his further purposes (as when he realizes that his further purpose would not be achieved by doing $X$ unless $C$ obtained). It is not sufficient for the agent's intention to do $X$ to be conditional with respect to $C$ that $C$ be a condition of the agent's doing $X$. It is also necessary that the agent believes that $C$ is a condition of his doing $X$. But this condition – that the agent believes that $C$ is a condition of his doing $X$ – while necessary, is also not itself sufficient for his intention to do $X$ being conditional with respect to $C$. The agent may well believe that his doing of $X$ is conditional upon the presence of $C$ and yet intend, unconditionally with respect to $C$, to do $X$. For the agent might very strongly believe that $C$ will be present at the proper time.

In order for the agent's intention to do $X$ to be conditional with respect to $C$, $C$ must satisfy the three conditions mentioned above, namely those pertaining to (i) the agent's changing his mind about doing $X$, (ii) his reasons for intending to do $X$, and (iii) his belief that he will try to do $X$. In addition, (iv) the agent must believe that his doing of $X$ depends upon the presence of $C$. I believe that these four conditions specify at least part of what it is for an intention to do $X$ to be conditional with respect to $C$. That is, these conditions specify at least part of what it is for $C$ to be part of what the agent intends or part of what the intention is about.

There are at least two other possible positions concerning conditional intentions. On the Conditional Object view – the view which I am maintaining – *actions in certain circumstances* can be objects of intentions and are objects of conditional intentions. On these other two views, actions in certain circumstances are not objects of conditional intentions. The first of these two other views may be called the 'Conditional Execution' view. According to this view, in a situation in which I have said that John conditionally intends to do $X$ if $C$ obtains, what John intends is to do $X$. But he also intends to execute or carry out this intention to do $X$ if $C$ obtains or, perhaps, only if $C$ obtains. The second position may be called the 'Conditional Decision' position. According to this second alternative view, in the situation in question, John comes to know that he wants to do $X$ and that he wants to do $X$

if $C$ obtains; and he decides that if $C$ obtains at some future time, he will decide at that *future* time to do $X$. On this view the agent decides, and therefore intends, to make *another* decision under certain circumstances. These views hold that the situations which I have claimed involve intentions having actions in certain circumstances as their objects are to be described in quite a different way.

### 3. *The Conditional Execution View*

The Conditional Execution view seems to be implausible as an alternative to the Conditional Object view. For the former mentions an intention that appears to have a conditional object. On the Conditional Execution view, the agent in fact has two intentions if he can truly be said to intend to do $X$ if $C$ obtains. The first intention is an intention to do $X$. The second intention is an intention to execute the first intention if $C$ obtains. And this second intention itself appears to be a conditional intention. Hence this view must show that this second intention is not a conditional intention if this view is to be an alternative to the Conditional Object view. What the Conditional Execution view is supposed to show is that situations apparently involving conditional intentions in fact involve only unconditional intentions. But, as we have just seen, the Conditional Execution view does not succeed in showing this.

Moreover, if the Conditional Execution view were correct, then an agent could have an intention to execute an intention to do $X$. But what would count as the execution of such an intention? Presumably this intention would be executed by doing $X$. For doing $X$ (while fulfilling other conditions to be discussed in Chapter 7) is to execute the intention to do $X$. And to execute the intention to do $X$ *is* to execute the intention to execute the intention to do $X$. Moreover, not to execute the former is not to execute the latter. So it seems that these two intentions are executed and not executed in exactly the same way. Now since I have adopted the criterion 'different descriptions, different intentions' (see Chapter 1, Section 2), I must count these as two different intentions. But although a person thus could have these two intentions, it is difficult to imagine a situation in which anyone would reasonably be said to have both of them. The job that would be taken care of by intending to execute the intention to do $X$ seems to be fully handled merely by intending to do $X$. So it is implausible for the

Conditional Execution View to attribute these two intentions to anyone.

I conclude that the Conditional Execution View does not offer a viable alternative to the Conditional Object Position. Now I turn to the other competitor of the latter, the Conditional Decision Position.

## 4. *The Conditional Decision Position*

According to the Conditional Decision position, when the agent decides to do $X$ if $C$ obtains, he has decided that if $C$ obtains, he will then decide to do $X$. But this does not redescribe the situation without mentioning conditional intentions either. For after deciding that if $C$ obtains, he will then decide to do $X$, the agent has a conditional intention to decide to do $X$ if $C$ obtains. That is, the condition is a condition of the agent's deciding to do $X$, not of his doing $X$. So the original conditional intention has been eliminated. For that original conditional intention was to do $X$ if $C$ obtains – where the condition is a condition of his *doing* $X$. But the original conditional intention has been replaced by another conditional intention in which the condition mentioned in the object of the intention is a condition of *deciding* to do $X$ rather than of doing $X$. Thus, this position is subject to the same type of difficulty as is the Conditional Execution position.

If the Conditional Object position is correct, then it follows that not all objects of intention are actions by themselves. For the conditional object 'to do $X$ if $C$ is present' has an action (namely, $X$) as a constituent but is not itself solely an action.

## 5. *Temporally Conditional Intentions*

A conditional intention is one in which the performance of the action is dependent, *in so far as what is intended is concerned*, on the agent's belief that a certain circumstance $X$ is present. *It is not the fact that the agent's performance of X does depend or even that it is believed by the agent to depend on the agent's having this belief that makes the intention a conditional intention*. For the agent's doing $X$ may depend and be believed to depend on his having this belief even in cases in which his intention is unconditional. For example, he might unconditionally intend to do $X$ because he believes that $C$ will be present; and in such a case his doing of $X$ may well depend in fact and be believed to depend on his having this belief. For he may change his mind about doing $X$ if he comes to believe that $C$ will not be present and he may know that he would do this. But this intention is still unconditional if his doing of $X$ being dependent on the presence of $C$ is not part of what he intends. *The difference between conditional intentions and unconditional intentions partly concerns, as we saw in Section 2, the conditions under which the agent will continue to have the intention in question, not the conditions under which he will perform the action.*

That this is not part of what the agent intends is, as we will see in Section 6, what allows his *having* of the unconditional intention to be conditional upon his belief that $C$ will obtain. And that this is part of what is intended in the conditional intention is what renders the *having* of that conditional intention independent of the agent's having this belief.

Now let us consider what I will call 'temporally conditional intentions'. These are intentions which are completely expressed by statements such as 'I intend to do $X$ at $t_i$.' The temporally conditional intention 'I intend to do $X$ at $t_i$' is similar to a conditional intention of the form 'to do $X$ if $C$ is present' in the following respect: in the case of each intention, the agent's doing of $X$ is dependent on the fulfilment of a certain condition and *in each case, that this is so is part of what is intended or part of what the intention is about.* In the case of the temporally conditional intention, the condition is that the moment be $t_i$.

This same similarity between conditional intentions and temporally conditional intentions can also be exhibited in the following way. Suppose the agent intends to do $X$ at $t_i$. But instead he does $X$ at a different time $t_j$. His doing $X$ at $t_j$ does not count as an execution of his intention to do $X$ at $t_i$; he did not do what he intended to do. Now suppose that the agent intends to do $X$ if $C$ obtains. $C$ never obtains, but at a certain time he does $X$. His doing of $X$ does not count as an execution of his intention if his intention is in fact a conditional intention – that is, an intention with a conditional content or a conditional object. It may seem that this is an execution of his intention. For it seems that we can truly say that he did what he intended to do. He intended to do $X$ and $X$ is what he did. But we can also say that he did not do $X$ in the circumstances in which he intended to do $X$. This is why his doing

23

$X$ is not an execution of his intention. This can be put in another way. The conditional intention 'to do $X$ if $C$ obtains' can also be expressed, at least partly, as the intention 'to do $X$ in circumstances $C$'. And only the performance of $X$ in those circumstances will count as an execution of this latter intention.

The agent does not carry out his intention to do $X$ if $C$ is present unless he does $X$ when $C$ is present. This shows in another way that the condition is part of what is intended when the agent has a conditional intention. If the agent only intends to do $X$ but not in any special circumstances – that is, has an unconditional intention to do $X$ – then he carries out his intention whenever he does $X$ intentionally regardless of the circumstances in which he does $X$. Even if he intended to do $X$ unconditionally because he believed that $C$ would be present, but did $X$ in circumstances $G$ instead while mistakenly believing that $C$ was present, he has nevertheless carried out his unconditional intention.

There is, however, a respect in which the intention to do $X$ at $t_i$ is not similar to the conditional intention to do $X$ if $C$ obtains. It seems to be a necessary condition of the agent's having the intention to do $X$ at $t_i$ that he believes that some future time will be $t_i$. He could, of course, intend to do $X$ at $t_i$ if $t_i$ is not already past, while believing that $t_i$ is already a past moment.[1] Thus, he would not believe that some future time will be $t_i$. But then this intention is a conditional intention and is not the temporally conditional intention to do $X$ at $t_i$. But it is certainly not a necessary condition of the agent's having the conditional intention to do $X$ if $C$ obtains that the agent believe that $C$ will obtain at some time. In fact, the agent may even be convinced that $C$ will never obtain and still intend to do $X$ if $C$ does obtain. So it seems that these two sorts of intentions differ with respect to the necessary conditions of an agent's having them.

Temporally conditional intentions are similar in the respect previously indicated to *conditional* intentions. But they are also similar to *unconditional* intentions in the following respect: when an agent intends to do $X$ (unconditionally) and also when he intends to do $X$ at $t_i$, he believes that he will do $X$ or try to do $X$ unless he changes his mind about this, comes to believe that there is no such action as '$X$', or is prevented from doing or trying to do $X$. But this is not the case

[1] The intention here has the form (to do $X$ at $t_i$ if $t_i$ is not already past).

24

with conditional intentions. As was said above, the agent who has such a conditional intention can nevertheless believe that $C$ will never obtain and hence can believe that he will never do $X$ or try to do $X$.

It is quite possible that in every case in which the agent makes a statement of intention such as 'I intend to do $X$', he must be prepared to say *when* it is that he will do $X$ or try to do $X$. If this is the case, then all non-conditional intentions are what I have called temporally conditional intentions; and all conditional intentions involve a temporal condition as well as non-temporal conditions. It is possible that all intentions involve temporal conditions – and perhaps that is not only so but necessarily so.

It is possible for an agent to express a conditional intention which involves a temporal condition without using the form 'at $t_i$' to do so. For when the agent says, 'I intend to do $X$ if $C$ is present,' he may mean that he intends to do $X$ if and when $C$ is present, and hence that he intends to do $X$ when $C$ is present. But there are two sorts of cases here. For if the agent were to say, 'I intend to do $X$ when $C$ is present,' he could mean that he intended to do $X$ at some time when $C$ is present or he could instead mean that he intended to do $X$ at the very next time that $C$ is present. If he meant the latter, then his intention would be temporally restricted or would involve a temporal condition. For only the performance of $X$ at a certain time at which $C$ is present will count as an execution of his intention. But if he means the former, there is no temporal restriction in the intention over and above the restriction imposed by his specifying that $C$ is a condition of his doing $X$. For if that is what he means, then his doing of $X$ at *any* time at which $C$ is present will count as an execution of his intention. However, to the extent to which the agent means the latter – that is, to the extent to which he means 'I intend to do $X$ at some time when $C$ is present' – it seems that the agent may well not be expressing an intention to do $X$ if $C$ is present, but only a wish or a desire to do $X$ if $C$ is present, just as he may well be expressing a wish or a desire to do $X$, rather than an intention to do $X$, when he says, 'I intend to do $X$ some day.'

## 6. *Types of Intentions and Reasons for Intending to do X*

In Section 2 I gave several reasons for believing that there are certain properties of intentions which I called 'conditionality' and 'unconditionality'. There I discussed the differences between conditional intentions and unconditional intentions with respect to the possible reasons which the agent might have for changing his mind about doing $X$ and with respect to the reasons which the agent would have for doing $X$. In Section 5 we also saw that these two types of intentions differ with respect to what would count as the execution or carrying out of an intention of each type. We also saw that there is a third property of intentions – temporal conditionality. It was said that these differences between conditional intentions and unconditional intentions exist because the type of thing that the agent intends is different in each case. In the case of an unconditional intention, the intention is about an action; and in the case of a conditional intention, the intention is about an action in certain circumstances. Each type of intention has a different type of object. Let us suppose that John believes that Fred Smith will run for president in the coming election year, and that George believes that if Fred Smith runs for president in the coming election year he will be elected. The proposition which John believes to be true has a different form from that which George believes to be true. It seems that the objects of these three types of intentions differ with respect to a property analogous to that of form for propositions. Just as different sorts of things count as confirmation or disconfirmation of propositions having different forms, so different sorts of things count as executions of intentions having objects of different 'forms'. The differences between these three types of intentions which were noted in Sections 2 and 5 exist because a different type of thing is intended in each of the three cases. The position that a different type of thing is intended in each case is what I have called the 'Conditional Object' position.

In this section I wish to discuss another difference between temporally conditional intentions and conditional intentions. This difference is also due to a difference in the kind of thing that is intended in each case.

Suppose that an agent believes that circumstances $C$ will obtain at a future time $t_i$ and is deliberating about whether or not to do $X$ at $t_i$ in these circumstances. He decides to do $X$ at $t_i$ in these circumstances, because he believes that $C$ will obtain at $t_i$ (and also believes that doing $X$ in $C$ will bring it about that $K$, $K$ being something which he desires to bring about). Does the agent, in the situation as described, have a conditional intention (to do $X$ at $t_i$ if $C$ obtains at $t_i$) or does he have a temporally conditional intention (to do $X$ at $t_i$)?

In the case as described – which we will call 'Case A' – the agent can give as his reason or one of his reasons for intending to do $X$ at $t_i$ that he believes that $C$ will be present at $t_i$. So our question is: in a case, such as Case A, in which the agent can give this type of reason for intending to do $X$ at $t_i$, does he have a conditional intention or a temporally conditional intention?

There is at least one type of case in which it seems that the agent can decide to do $X$ at $t_i$ or come to have the intention of doing $X$ at $t_i$ because certain circumstances are believed by the agent to be present at $t_i$ and yet in which it is incorrect to regard this intention as a conditional intention. These are cases in which the agent is deliberating about what to do 'right away' or at the very next instant or as soon as he completes his deliberations. In such cases, the agent may intend to do $X$ at the next moment because he believes that $C$ will then prevail or will continue to prevail; but he knows that there will be no time between his decision and his performance of $X$ during which he could come to have a different belief about what circumstances are present at $t_i$. So it seems that in such cases his doing of $X$ at $t_i$, though dependent on his belief that $C$ prevails at $t_i$, is not dependent on this belief in the same way as it is in what we have been calling 'conditional intentions'. In this case he is committed to doing $X$ at $t_i$. In the previous cases he was committed to doing $X$ at $t_i$ if or *only if* he had certain beliefs at a certain future time. He was conditionally committed to doing $X$ at $t_i$. But in the present case he is fully committed to doing $X$ at $t_i$. In fact, the agent may have a conditional intention to do $X$ at some future time $t_i$ and then, at the moment before $t_i$, come to have a temporally conditional intention of the sort being discussed because he believes that $C$ will obtain at $t_i$ and knows that there will be no time in which to come to have a different belief about what circumstances will prevail at $t_i$. Temporally conditional intentions are perhaps always associated with conditional intentions in this way – that at a certain point in time before the performance of $X$, the agent who has a conditional intention ceases to have that conditional intention and comes to have a temporally conditional intention with respect to the same action. The agent will then do $X$ at $t_i$ *because* he has a certain belief about circumstances, rather than will do $X$ at $t_i$ *if* he has that belief. Though his doing of $X$ at $t_i$ depends in both cases on his having that belief, his attitude towards and commitment to do $X$ at $t_i$ differs in these two intentions in the ways just indicated. Thus, there is a type of case – namely, the type in which the agent must do the action at the next moment – in which the agent intends to do $X$ because he believes that $C$ is or will be present and his intention is a temporally conditional intention rather than a conditional intention. This supports the view that in Case A the agent's intention is a temporally conditional intention, since the agents in these two types of cases have the same reason for intending to do $X$ at $t_i$ and thus have the same attitude towards $C$.

Now let us consider cases in which the agent is not necessarily going to do $X$ at the very next moment. An important difference between conditional intentions and temporally conditional intentions is this. An agent may say, 'I intend to do $X$ at $t_i$,' and when asked why he does so, may say, 'I intend to do $X$ at $t_i$ because I believe that $C$ will obtain at $t_i$.' Here the agent is giving a partial explanation of the fact that he *has* a certain intention. If his intention were a conditional intention – 'to do $X$ at $t_i$ if $C$ obtains' – he could not explain in the same way why he has the conditional intention. He could not say, 'I intend to do $X$ at $t_i$ if $C$ obtains because I believe that $C$ will obtain at $t_i$.' For this would be no explanation at all. He would explain his having this conditional intention by saying, 'I intend to do $X$ at $t_i$ if $C$ obtains because I believe that the doing of $X$ in $C$ at $t_i$ will bring it about that $K$ and I want to bring it about that $K$.' Of course, in the first case – that in which the agent explains *his having an intention* to do $X$ at $t_i$ by citing his belief that certain circumstances will prevail – the agent could also mention that doing $X$ at $t_i$ in the presence of $C$ will or is believed to bring it about that $K$. However, in mentioning the putative relation between the presence of $C$ and the bringing about of $K$, the agent would there be explaining not only why he intends to do $X$ at $t_i$ but also *why his belief that $C$ will obtain is a reason for intending to do $X$ at $t_i$.* But in the second case – the case in which he intends to do $X$ at $t_i$ if $C$ obtains – he cannot cite his belief *that $C$ will obtain* as a reason for intending to do $X$ at $t_i$ if $C$ does obtain; it is his citing of the putative relation between the presence of $C$ and the bringing about of $K$ that

28

would instead constitute an explanation of why he intends to do $X$ at $t_i$ if $C$ obtains. That is, in the second case the citing of this putative relation between doing $X$ in $C$ and $K$ plays the same role as does the citing of his belief about whether $C$ will obtain plays in the first case. This indicates that two different types of intentions are involved in these two cases. *If the agent's intention were a conditional intention to do X at $t_i$ if C obtains, then he could not explain his having the intention which he has by saying that he has that intention because he believes that C will obtain at $t_i$. Thus, we may take as a sufficient condition of an intention's being a temporally conditional intention with respect to circumstances C the agent's citing his belief that circumstances C will obtain as a reason why he intends to do X at $t_i$.*

It might be objected that an agent could explain his having the intention of doing $X$ at $t_i$ if $C$ obtains by saying that he believes that circumstances $C_1$ will obtain at $t_i$, and if $C$ also obtains at $t_i$, then the combination of $C$ and $C_1$ will constitute the proper circumstances in which to do $X$. Here the agent does express a belief that circumstances $C_1$ will obtain at $t_i$ in the course of explaining why he has a certain intention, and yet that intention is a conditional intention. So beliefs that circumstances will obtain can be expressed in explaining the having of conditional intentions. Therefore, that such beliefs can or cannot be expressed in such explanations does not differentiate conditional from temporally conditional intentions.

It is true that such beliefs can be expressed in such explanations. But nevertheless the circumstances ($C_1$) which it is believed will occur at $t_i$ do not form part of the condition of the conditional intention. The condition of the above conditional intention is 'if $C$ obtains', not 'if $C_1$ obtains'. The conditional intention is non-conditional with respect to $C_1$, even though it is a conditional intention with respect to $C$. That is, $C_1$ does not occur as part of what is intended in the way in which $C$ does in this intention. I have spoken of intentions as being conditional or non-conditional *with respect to specific sets of circumstances*. An intention cannot merely be said to be conditional; it must also be specified with respect to what circumstances it is conditional. An intention is conditional with respect to circumstances $C$ if $C$ is part of the condition; if $C$ is not part of the condition, that intention is non-conditional with respect to $C$, even if it is conditional with respect to some other circumstances. It was said above that beliefs that certain circumstances will obtain can be expressed as part of an explanation of an agent's having a given intention only if that intention is unconditional or temporally conditional. But in view of the above, what must be said is that such beliefs can be expressed in such explanations only if the intention in question is non-conditional *with respect to the circumstances mentioned in the expression of such beliefs.*

Taking the way in which the agent would explain his having of the intention in question as a criterion of what type of intention it is provides us with a way of determining what type of intention a given intention is that is independent of the logical form of the sentence by uttering which that intention is expressed. Furthermore, this criterion is also independent of whether or not a particular circumstance is mentioned by the agent in expressing his intention. That a certain sort of explanation can be given of the agent's having a given intention is to be explained by showing that *what is intended* is of a certain sort or has a certain form. This is why the type of explanation given of having a certain intention can serve as a criterion of what type of intention it is. Regardless of the form which a sentence used in making a statement of intention might have, if the agent cites his belief that $C$ will obtain at $t_i$ as an explanation of his intending to do $X$ at $t_i$, then to that extent the agent has a non-conditional (in this case a temporally conditional) intention with respect to $C$ or an intention in which $C$ is not a condition or part of the object. For that his intention does not include 'if $C$ obtains' as a condition explains why he can cite *this* belief as such an explanation. And that this is so shows in another way that conditional intentions on the one hand and intentions (such as temporally conditional intentions and unconditional intentions) which are non-conditional on the other are quite different types of intentions.

In Case A (described at the beginning of this section), the agent can give as one of his reasons for intending to do $X$ at $t_i$. that he believes that $C$ will be present at $t_i$. This shows that he has a temporally conditional intention to do $X$ at $t_i$ which is non-conditional with respect to $C$, since the intention for the having of which he gives such a reason cannot be conditional with respect to $C$, as we have seen.

Does the agent in Case A also have a conditional intention to do $X$ at $t_i$ in addition to his temporally conditional intention to do $X$ at $t_i$? Is it even possible for the agent to have two such intentions at the same time? First, we must distinguish between two types of conditional intentions. The first type is expressed by the statement 'He intends to do

*X if C* is present' and may be called an 'inclusive conditional intention'. The second type is expressed by the statement 'He intends to do *X only if C* is present' and may be called an 'exclusive conditional intention'. It is clear that the agent can have an intention to do $X$ at $t_i$ which is non-conditional with respect to $C$ and at the same time an intention to do $X$ at $t_i$ which is inclusively conditional with respect to some circumstance other than $C$ (call it $G$). For he can intend to do $X$ at $t_i$ because he believes that $C$ will be present at $t_i$ and simultaneously intend to do $X$ at $t_i$ if $G$ is present instead of $C$, even though he believes that $G$ will not be present. But he cannot have such a temporally conditional intention (to do $X$ at $t_i$) which is non-conditional with respect to $C$ and at the same time have an intention to do $X$ at $t_i$ which is exclusively conditional with respect to $G$. For he cannot intend to do $X$ at $t_i$ (because, for example, he believes that $C$ will be present at $t_i$) and simultaneously intend to do $X$ at $t_i$ only if $G$ is present at $t_i$. What could he mean by saying, 'I intend to do $X$ at $t_i$ because $C$ will be present and I intend to do $X$ at $t_i$ only if $G$ is present?'

Let us now turn from the case of different circumstances $C$ and $G$ to the case of just one circumstance $C$. Can the agent have an intention to do $X$ at $t_i$ which is non-conditional with respect to $C$ and at the same time an intention to do $X$ at $t_i$ which is conditional with respect to that *same* circumstance $C$? The agent can have both intentions if the conditional intention is an exclusive conditional intention. For the agent can intend to do $X$ at $t_i$ because he believes that $C$ will be present at $t_i$ and at the same time intend to do $X$ at $t_i$ only if $C$ is present at $t_i$. This case is not as clear as the one just considered. It depends on whether the agent can sensibly say, 'I intend to do $X$ at $t_i$ because $C$ will be present but I intend to do $X$ at $t_i$ only if C is present.' It seems to me that the agent can sensibly say this. If so, then the agent can have an intention which is at one and the same time non-conditional with respect to $C$ and exclusively conditional with respect to $C$. It may also seem that the agent could also intend to do $X$ at $t_i$ because he believes that $C$ will be present at $t_i$ and at the same time intend to do $X$ at $t_i$ if $C$ is present at $t_i$. That is, it may seem that the agent can also have both intentions if the conditional intention is inclusively conditional. But what would the agent be saying if he said, 'I intend to do $X$ at $t_i$ and I intend to do $X$ at $t_i$ if $C$ is present at $t_i$.' The second conjunct of his statement seems to qualify the first in such a way that he is saying that he has *only* an inclusive conditional intention to do $X$ at $t_i$. All that he could otherwise mean by such a statement is that he not only intends to do $X$ at $t_i$ but also intends to do $X$ at $t_i$ only if $C$ is present at $t_i$; but this is not to have both a temporally conditional intention and an inclusive conditional intention directed towards the same action with respect to the same circumstance. For if this is what he means, then his conditional intention is *exclusively* conditional.

It might be objected that since I have already claimed that the agent can have the temporally conditional intention at the same time as having the exclusively conditional intention, and since an agent cannot have the latter without having the inclusively conditional intention as well, he can therefore have the temporally conditional intention at the same time as he has the *inclusively* conditional intention. But this is not so. First, an agent can have an exclusively conditional intention without having the corresponding inclusively conditional intention. He can have made up his mind to go to New York only if Jones is there – that is, not to go if Jones is not there – without yet having made up his mind to go if Jones is there. Second, what was said in the previous paragraph shows that when the agent does make up his mind to go if Jones is there, he no longer has (if indeed he ever had) the corresponding temporally conditional intention.

Thus, in Case A, the agent cannot have an inclusive conditional intention with respect to $C$ (to do $X$ at $t_i$ if $C$ is present at $t_i$) since he does have an intention to do $X$ at $t_i$ which is non-conditional with respect to $C$. He could, however, have a conditional intention to do $X$ at $t_i$ which is exclusively conditional with respect to $C$.

## 7. Conditionality, Unconditionality, and Belief

In the preceding sections I have tried to show in several different ways that there is a difference between conditionality and unconditionality of intentions. This was shown by discussing the grounds which the agent could have for changing his mind about doing $X$ (Section 2), the kinds of reasons which the agent can give for intending to do $X$ (Section 6), and so on. This establishes that there are such things as conditionality of intention and unconditionality of intention and that these are different from one another.

I have further tried to explain why these differences exist by saying that the objects of intention are different in each case. That is, what is intended is different in each case. If the agent's intention to do $X$ is conditional with respect to $C$, then what he intends is *to do X if C obtains*; if the agent's intention is not conditional with respect to some $C$, then what the agent intends is *to do X*.

Now I want to suggest at least one reason, if not the only reason, why the object of the agent's intention is different in each case. That is, this is a reason why the agent's intention is conditional with respect to $C$ or unconditional with respect to $C$. I suggest that whether or not an agent's intention to do $X$ at $t_4$ is conditional with respect to $C$ depends, at least partly, on what he believes or does not believe about *the chances of C's being present at $t_4$*. If the agent believes that his doing of $X$ at $t_4$ depends on $C$'s being present at $t_4$ (because, for example, he believes that only if $C$ is present will the performance of $X$ at $t_4$ bring it about that $K$), then the following is the case: if the agent in addition strongly believes that $C$ will be present at $t_4$, then his intention is unconditional with respect to $C$ – what he intends is to do $X$ at $t_4$; if the agent does not, in addition, strongly believe that $C$ will be present at $t_4$, then his intention is conditional with respect to $C$ – what he intends is to do $X$ at $t_4$ if $C$ is present at $t_4$. Of course, if the agent has no beliefs about the relation between $C$ and his doing $X$, his intention is unconditional with respect to $C$. $C$ plays no role in what he intends.

Someone might object to this suggestion by saying that a person's intention can be conditional with respect to $C$ even if the person knows that $C$ will occur. For example, a person might say, 'If it rains, I'll stay at home,' even though he knows that it will rain. I agree that a person might say this even though he knows that it will rain. But I do not believe that this statement would express the person's intention. It seems to me that the person would be committed to staying at home. He would have decided to stay at home in view of the fact that it will rain. Of course, he may still have certain reasons for indicating (falsely) to his hearers that his intention is conditional. But what he says here does not accurately express his intention.

It must be emphasized that an intention's being unconditional with respect to $C$ is not dependent on the agent's not knowing or believing that his performance of $X$ at $t_4$ is dependent upon $C$'s presence at $t_4$ (or his belief that $C$ is present at $t_4$). Nor is it identical with the agent's not mentioning $C$ in expressing his intention even if he does know or believe this. The agent can know that his performance of $X$ at $t_4$ depends on his believing at $t_4$ that $C$ is present and still intend to do $X$

at $t_4$ unconditionally with respect to $C$. And he can fail to mention $C$ in expressing his intention and still have that intention be one which is conditional with respect to $C$. What determines the role which $C$ plays in his intention is, in part, I suggest, his beliefs (or lack thereof) about the relation between $C$ and his doing $X$ and his belief about the chances of $C$'s being present at $t_4$.

# 3 The objects of intention

## 1. *Introduction*

The expression 'object of an intention' will be used in this chapter, as it was in Chapter 2, to refer to what a given intention is about or what is intended when an agent has a given intention. Thus, if the agent intends to go to New York, the object of his intention is the action 'going to New York'.

In this chapter I will discuss certain central questions about objects of intention. Section 2 deals with the question: what sorts of things can serve as objects of intentions? Later sections also concern possible restrictions on objects of intention. Thus, in Section 4 we consider whether an action must be logically possible in order to be a possible object of intention. And in Section 5 it is discussed whether a necessary condition of a given action's being a possible object of intention for a given agent is that that agent know what it is to perform that action. In the final section, the notion of a compound object of intention is introduced and discussed.

## 2. *The Actions Theses*

What sorts of things can be intended? To put this same question in another way, what sorts of objects can intentions have?

Clearly, actions of the agent who expresses the intentions in question can be objects of those intentions. For example, the agent may say, 'I intend to go downtown tomorrow' or 'I intend to arrange the meeting for Friday.' But actions of the agent who expresses the intentions in question are not the only possible objects of those intentions. An agent may also say, 'I intend to become the next U.S. Representative from this district.' Here the object of the agent's intention is an event. This event may be brought about by the agent's own actions, but this event is not itself an action. Thus, events that are not actions can be objects of intentions.

Two other locutions (besides 'I intend to . . .') used in expressing or

35

reporting intentions are 'I intend that . . .' and 'My intention is that . . .'. For example, the owner of a taxicab company might say to his drivers: 'I intend that there be two cabs at this station at all times.' Here the object of intention is a state of affairs – two cabs at a certain place at all times. To take another example, suppose that an organization appoints a committee to draw up a new constitution for that organization. The officers might say to the committee: 'It is our intention that your committee draw up a new constitution.' And when reporting back to the officers, the committee chairman might say: 'It is our intention that this document serve as the new constitution.' This shows that actions of others (that the committee draw up the new constitution) and states of affairs (this document's serving as the new constitution) can be objects of intentions. Thus, actions of the agent himself, actions of others, events that are not actions, and states of affairs can all be objects of intention. They can be what is intended, what intentions are about, or what the agent's intention is directed towards.

But even though things that are not actions of the agent who has a given intention can be objects of that intention, nevertheless the following principle is true:

> If an agent has an intention whose object is something $K$ (for example, a state of affairs) that is not an action of that agent himself, then the agent must also have another intention or set of intentions – he must also intend *to do X*, where '$X$' stands for some action or actions of the agent himself. Moreover, $X$ must be such that the agent believes that to do $X$ will not only have some role in bringing it about that $K$, but also that to do $X$ is at least to go quite a distance towards bringing it about that $K$.

We will call this 'the First Actions Thesis'. It is also true, as Miss Anscombe has said, that a statement can express the intention with which the agent does some action $X$ only if we can understand the agent's thinking that the state of affairs mentioned in the statement will or can be brought about by something that the agent will or might do.[1] Let us call this 'the Anscombe Thesis'. The Anscombe Thesis is quite different from the First Actions Thesis. First, the Anscombe Thesis states a necessary condition of any sort of object's being the object of an intention, while the First Actions Thesis states a necessary condition of a certain type of object's being the object of an intention. Sec-

[1] G. E. M. Anscombe, *Intention* (Oxford, 1958), p. 35.

ond, these asserted necessary conditions are quite different from one another. Most important, the First Actions Thesis claims that the agent's action must be *intended* by that agent, not merely believed by the agent to be connected with the intended state of affairs.

According to the First Actions Thesis, a necessary condition of the agent's having an intention directed towards an object that is not one of his own actions is that he also have an intention which is directed towards one or more of his own actions and this action or actions be believed by the agent to have a certain relation to that other object of intention.

Let us consider again the case of the committee that is drawing up the new constitution. One possible situation is that (i) two weeks after the committee adopts some document, that document automatically becomes the new constitution of the organization, provided that the committee does not vote again and differently in that two-week interval. Another possible situation is that (ii) after the committee approves a document, that document must then be approved by six other committees, by the governing body of the organization, and by all of the organizations affiliated with that organization; moreover, if any one of these other committees and organizations disapproves the document, then that document cannot become the new constitution. In situation (i), it would be possible for the chairman of the first committee to say truly, 'We intend that this document be our new constitution.' But it would not be possible for him to say this truly in situation (ii) unless he believes that the other committees and organizations will approve any document accepted by his committee or he believes that his committee can persuade the others to approve their document. Unless he has these beliefs or other beliefs of this type, he cannot truly say, 'We intend that this document be our new constitution.' He can only say, 'We would like this document to be our new constitution' or 'We hope that this document will be our new constitution.'

This can be shown in another way. Let $E$ be an event. Suppose that Jones says that he intends that $E$ should have occurred or that $E$ had occurred. Jones can hope that $E$ occurred. He can find out whether or not $E$ has occurred at some past time; and if he finds that $E$ has not occurred, he can wish that $E$ had occurred. But he cannot intend that $E$ should have occurred unless he believes that there is some action which he can now or later perform and which will affect the past in such a way as to go quite a distance towards bringing about the past occurrence of $E$. If he believes that he can affect the past in this way,

37

then he can intend that $E$ should have occurred, even if he cannot in fact affect the past in this way. If he does not have such a belief about some of his own actions, then he cannot intend this. He can merely hope or wish with respect to the past. If someone were to say that he intends that some past event should have occurred, most people would wonder whether the agent knew how to use the word 'intend'. And the reason why they would do this is that they believe very strongly not only that no one can bring about something in the past or cause something to have happened but also that no one believes that he can affect the past in this way. Thus, the First Actions Thesis helps to explain why it is commonly believed that one cannot intend that some past event have happened.

If there were time machines capable of allowing men to travel into the past and if men could use these machines to affect the past, then statements that the agent intends that a past event should have occurred would be perfectly acceptable. But such statements would become acceptable only because men would then be able to affect the past – that is, to perform actions which can help quite a bit to bring it about that such an event have occurred. And that this is so supports the First Actions Thesis.

Suppose that an agent is building a small aeroplane. He says that he intends that this plane should be capable of speeds up to two hundred and fifty miles per hour. But if he goes on to say that there is nothing he can possibly do to endow the plane with this capability, we would wonder why he used the term 'intend'. It is not that his statement of intention is meaningless; we know what he is trying to convey. But we would wonder why he used the term 'intend' when one of the necessary conditions of using 'intend' in that way was not satisfied. Similarly, people do not intend that a certain volcano not erupt. And this is not because the non-eruption of the volcano is not important to them. It is instead because they believe that they can do nothing or very little to affect the volcano's behaviour. But not only *do* they not have such intentions because of this; they *cannot* have such intentions because of this. Only if they believe that they can affect the volcano's behaviour *can* they have such intentions.

I have given one type of argument for the First Actions Thesis. It might now be objected that there can be a type of case in which at a certain time $t_1$ the agent intends that $K$ and yet at that same time he does not intend to perform any action $X$ having the proper relation to

$K$. For example, at $t_1$ the agent may intend that something $S$ be done in a certain way both at $t_1$ and from then on; and in fact the agent does various things to bring this about. But at $t_4$, though he still intends that $S$ continue to be done in that way at $t_4$, $t_5$, and so on, either (1) he believes that it is not necessary for him to do anything to bring this about (perhaps because he believes that his previous action has brought this about) or (2) he is not and knows that he is not in a position to do anything to bring this about. So at $t_4$ he does not intend to perform an action which he believes will bring it about that $S$ continues to be done in a certain way. Thus, although at $t_4$ he intends that $S$ be done in that way at $t_4$, $t_5$, and so on, he does not intend at $t_4$ to perform an action of the required sort.

It is true that this agent does not have what we might call a categorical intention at $t_4$ to perform an action of the required sort. But he does have a conditional intention to do so. To take (1) first, he must intend at $t_4$ to do something that will bring it about that $S$ is done in this way if it is necessary for him to do so in order that $S$ be done in this way. In a similar way, a conditional intention is involved in (2): he intends at $t_4$ to do something to bring it about that $S$ is done in this way if there is anything which needs to be done and can be done by him for this purpose.

The Second Actions Thesis is this:

It is a necessary condition of the agent's intending something $K$ which is not an action of his own (for example, a state of affairs) that the agent intend to bring it about that $K$.

The First Actions Thesis requires that the agent intend to do something $X$ which he believes will go quite a distance towards bringing it about that $K$, in order to intend that $K$. The Second Actions Thesis requires that the agent also intend *to bring it about that $K$*. Let us consider again the case of the man building the aeroplane. Suppose that we ask him whether he has done anything to make the plane capable of going the speed he intends it to be capable of. If he says that he has not done so, and further says that he does not intend to bring this about, we would wonder why he claims to intend that it be capable of that speed. If the constitutional committee chairman does not intend to see to it that the other committees and organizations approve his document and thus that it become the new constitution, then he does not intend this document to be the new constitution. Suppose that the aeroplane builder said: 'I intend that this plane be such that it can fly at two hundred and fifty miles per hour and I believe that I can construct it in such a way that it will be capable of this, but I do not intend to do so or to do anything which will bring it about that it is constructed in this way.' It would be most appropriate to reply: 'You mean instead that you expect that it will turn out to have that capacity or that you hope that it will turn out this way.'

The Second Actions Thesis can also be put in terms of the notion of an intrinsic element of an action. Let us define 'intrinsic element of action $X$' in the following way:

A state of affairs, event, and so on (let us call it '$K$') is an intrinsic element of an action $X$ if and only if the agent's bringing $K$ about is a logically necessary condition of his having performed $X$.

For example, the event of the agent's reaching the top of a given mountain is an intrinsic element of the action of his climbing the mountain. An action may have more than one intrinsic element. And one intrinsic element may be an intrinsic element of more than one action. Some intrinsic elements are also intrinsic ends. For they not only occur at the end of the action in question but also constitute the culmination of that action. $K$ is an intrinsic end of $X$ if, and only if, it is both an end of $X$ and an intrinsic element of $X$. For example, reaching the top of the mountain is not only an intrinsic element of the action of climbing a mountain; it is also an intrinsic end of that action.

Does every action have at least one intrinsic element? Let us consider the action of running, since running presumably has no intrinsic end. An agent need not have moved from one place to another in order to have run, nor need he intend to do so in order to intend to run. For one is running when one is 'running in place' or 'running on the spot'. But the agent must move certain parts of his body from certain locations or positions to certain other locations or positions in order to have run. And it seems that therefore 'the limbs being in different positions at different times' is intrinsic to the action of running. This does satisfy the criterion previously stated of being an intrinsic element of running.[1]

[1] Many actions have intrinsic elements. Some actions which have intrinsic elements also have what we might call 'intrinsic intentions'. Let us suppose, for example, that an agent is uttering French words. In order for this activity to count as the agent's practising his French pronunciation, the agent must not only utter French words – the utterance of such words being the intrinsic ele-

The Second Actions Thesis can now be put in the following way: If $K$ is some state of affairs, event, or action of another, then the agent can intend that $K$ if, and only if, he intends to perform an action of which $K$ is an intrinsic element, namely the action 'bringing it about that $K$' or the action 'helping to bring it about that $K$'.

This formulation of the Second Actions Thesis is in terms of 'bringing it about that $K$'. 'Bringing it about that $K$' seems to be an action which is related to some action or actions $X$ in the same way in which the action of signalling is related to other actions. When an automobile driver moves his arm in a certain way and with a certain intention, he is signalling. He is signalling *by* raising his arm or he is signalling *in* raising his arm. Similarly, the agent brings it about that $K$ *by* performing $X$ or as in the case of running and the agent's limbs being in various positions, *in* performing $K$. It is true that the agent cannot do something which is solely describable as 'bringing it about that $K$'; if the agent does something which is describable in this way, then what he does *must* be describable in at least one other way also. But this fact – which we may perhaps express by saying that 'bringing it about that $K$' is a higher-order description – does not show that 'bringing it about that $K$' is not a description of an action. For the description 'signalling' is clearly a description of an action, and yet the agent cannot signal without doing something which can also be described in some way other than as signalling.

If we adopt the view that 'bringing it about that $K$' is a description of an action, then we must say either that (i) this description is a description of the same action of which the expression '$X$' is a description (where the agent brings it about that $K$ by or in doing $X$) or else that (ii) 'bringing it about that $K$' is a description of a different action from that of which '$X$' is a description. If we adopt (i), then an action can be described in a way which does not show that one of its intrinsic elements is indeed one of its intrinsic elements. For example, let '$X$' stand for 'asking John to go to New York'. 'That John goes to New York' is certainly not an intrinsic element of asking John to go to New York, whereas it would in fact be such an intrinsic element if (i) is adopted.

---

ment related to the action 'practising French pronunciation' – but he must also have a certain intention in so doing. He must intend to improve his French pronunciation. An intention the having of which is a logically necessary condition of performing an action $X$ is what we may call an 'intrinsic intention' of action $X$.

For on (i) there is only one action in this situation. This element is, on (i), an intrinsic element of 'bringing it about that John goes to New York' and hence of the action 'asking John to go to New York'. For on (i) these two descriptions are both descriptions of *one* action. But surely, the agent can ask John to go to New York without bringing it about that John does so. So, that John goes to New York is not an intrinsic element of asking John to go to New York. Thus, it does not seem plausible to say that the former is an intrinsic element of the latter, as we would have to do on alternative (i). For this reason, it seems preferable to adopt alternative (ii) and to treat the description 'bringing it about that $K$' as a description of an action which is distinct from $X$ even though the agent cannot perform the former action without performing *some* action $X$. Thus, when the agent brings it about that $K$ by doing $X$, he performs at least two distinct actions.

## 2. *Is Intending that K Identical with Intending to Bring It About that K?*

If the Second Actions Thesis is correct, then intending to bring it about that $K$ is a necessary condition of intending that $K$. The former also seems to be a sufficient condition of the latter. First, it seems that George could not have decided to bring it about and therefore have the intention of bringing it about that John goes to New York next week without intending that John shall go to New York next week. What could he mean by affirming that he has the first intention and denying that he has the second? Second, suppose that George intends that John shall go to New York but then changes his mind about this. Before George changed his mind about this, he intended that John shall go to New York. And therefore, if the Second Actions Thesis is correct, before he changed his mind about this, he also intended to bring it about that John goes to New York. So at a certain point in time before he changed his mind about this – let us call this moment '$t_1$' – the agent had two intentions: he intended that $K$ and he intended to bring it about that $K$. Then at a later time $t_2$, the agent changed his mind with respect to the object of the first intention. After $t_2$ he no longer intended that John shall go to New York and perhaps even intended that John shall not go to New York. But then, after $t_2$, he cannot still intend to bring it about that $K$. That is, he cannot not intend that John shall go to New York and at the same time intend to bring it about that John goes to New York. But he does not also have to change his mind about bringing it about that John goes to New York, in addition to changing his mind about whether John shall go to New York. He need not change his mind about each of these. For after he ceases to intend that *K*, he *thereby* does not continue to intend to bring it about that *K*. Changing his mind about the former, and hence no longer intending that *K*, is sufficient for no longer intending to bring it about that *K*. Therefore, intending to bring it about that *K* is a sufficient condition of intending that *K*.

Thus, intending to bring it about that *K* is a necessary and sufficient condition of intending that *K*. But this does not show that these intentions are identical with one another. According to the principle of individuation of intentions which I adopted in Section 2 of Chapter 1, namely 'different descriptions, different intentions', these intentions are not identical with one another. For we have here a case of two different descriptions and hence two different, though closely related, intentions.

If an intention that *K* could be shown to be nothing more than an intention to bring it about that *K*, then this would give substantial support to what we might call 'the Objects Thesis':

> Only actions are objects of intentions.

For the object of the intention that *K* would be not the state of affairs *K*, but instead the action 'bringing it about that *K*'. The Objects Thesis is, of course, quite different from the thesis that every intention has an object.

## 3. *Intending the Impossible*

What restrictions, if any, are there on the possibility of something's being an object of an intention? The particular question pertaining to this topic which I wish to discuss in this section is: Must an action be logically possible in order for it to be possible for an agent to intend to perform that action?

Let us suppose that the letter '*X*' stands for or is to be replaced by a description of a logically impossible action – for instance, 'drawing an elliptical pentagon' or 'capturing a unicorn having two horns'. By 'logically impossible action' here, I mean 'an action which cannot be done *because* its description (perhaps together with certain necessary truths) contains or entails a contradiction'. Can the agent intend to perform such an action? For example, can an agent intend to draw an elliptical pentagon? It might be denied that the agent can intend this on the following grounds. Intentions are distinguished from one another by their objects. The intention to go to Chicago is different from the intention to go to New York just because the action 'going to Chicago' is different from the action 'going to New York'. But there are no such things as logically impossible actions. The expressions which seem to be descriptions of logically impossible actions are instead descriptions of nothing at all. So intentions which seem to be directed at such actions have no objects at all. But if there can be intentions that have no objects, then how could they differ from one another? How could the intention to draw an elliptical pentagon differ from the intention to capture a two-horned unicorn? If these intentions cannot differ from one another, then at most there is just one intention that has no object and all other supposed intentions that have no objects are identical with this one intention. It might further be said that a second reason for denying that the agent can intend to draw an elliptical pentagon is this. Such a supposed intention is an intention that cannot be carried out or executed or even acted in accordance with. But how can there be an intention that cannot even be acted in accordance with? Moreover, it might be said that a third reason for denying that the agent can intend to square the circle is as follows. It seems appropriate to speak of an agent as trying to do $X$ only in cases in which he can succeed in doing $X$. If so, then the agent cannot appropriately be said to be trying to draw an elliptical pentagon, for he cannot succeed in drawing an elliptical pentagon. Therefore, if he can intend to draw an elliptical pentagon, he can intend to do something that he cannot even try to do. Yet there seems to be a very close connection between intending and trying – so close as to rule out the possibility that the agent can intend to do something that he cannot try to do.

But the difficulty with denying that the agent can intend to perform an action which is in fact logically impossible is that intending to perform such an action seems to be exactly what some people have done. For example, certain early mathematicians seemed to have tried to square the circle. And if an agent tries to do $X$, he intends to do $X$. Thus, the description 'intending to square the circle' seems to be a description which can be correctly applied to these mathematicians.

There are several replies that can be made to this. The first reply is that what these mathematicians were trying to do was not to square the circle but instead to find out whether or not the circle could be squared. Nevertheless, it does seem possible for a mathematician who does not know or believe that it is logically impossible to square the circle to say sincerely, 'I intend to square the circle.' But it may now be replied that in every statement of intention, there is always an implicit rider of the form 'if it is logically possible to do so'. Thus, the mathematician would be understood as saying, 'I intend to square the circle if it is logically possible to do so.' This reply is intended to support the view that one cannot intend to do what is logically impossible. But this reply would be satisfactory only if the logical possibility of performing the action in question is a condition of the agent's *having the intention of* performing the action rather than only a condition of the agent's *performing* the action. The rider concerning logical possibility could mean 'If this action is logically possible, then I intend to perform it; but I do not intend to perform it if it is not logically possible.' But this rider could also mean 'I intend to perform this action and will perform it if the action is logically possible; if the action is not logically possible, then I still intend to perform it for I do not now know whether or not it is logically possible, but in fact I will not perform it because I will not be able to perform it.' Only if the logical possibility of performing the action were a condition of *having the intention of* performing that action would the necessity of adding this rider support the view that an agent cannot intend to perform a logically impossible action. For if the logical possibility of performing the action were instead only a condition of *performing* the action, the agent could still *intend* to perform that action even if it were logically impossible for the action to be performed.

It seems that it is not the logical possibility of performing the action but instead the lack of belief by the agent that the action is logically impossible that is a condition of the agent's having the intention of performing that action. It is not the case that if the action is not logically possible, the agent cannot intend to perform that action. Instead, it is the case that if the agent comes to believe that the action is logically impossible, he can no longer intend to do it. What could be meant by a contemporary mathematician who says that he intends to square the circle and also claims to believe that it is not logically possible to square the circle?

So there are two reasons why adding the rider 'if it is logically possible to do so' to statements of intention does not succeed in show-ing that the agent cannot intend to perform a logically impossible action. (i) The rider may state only a condition of *performing* the action rather than also a condition of *having the condition of* performing the action. (ii) What seems to be a condition of having the intention of performing the action is not the action's being logically possible but instead the agent's *not believing* that the action is logically impossible. For it is only when the agent believes the action to be logically impossible that we would not understand his saying, 'I intend to perform that action,' whereas we would understand this if he, for example, believed the action to be logically possible even if this belief is false.

The statement 'Certain early mathematicians intended to square the circle' seems to be true. And we have just seen that objection to the position that an agent cannot intend to do an action that is logically impossible cannot be answered by the use of riders of the form 'if it can be done'. It was objected earlier in this section, that there can be no intentions to do the logically impossible. For there are no such things as logically impossible actions. Hence, all such intentions would have at most the same object and hence not be different from one another. The beginning of a reply to this objection might go as fol-lows. First the agent knows what would count as squaring the circle, namely various operations with ruler and compasses which resulted in a square having the same area as a given circle. And he knows what would count as, for example, trisecting an angle. Since a different process would count as the execution of the intention to square the circle from the process which would count as executing the intention of trisecting an angle, these two intentions are different. This can also be put in terms of necessary conditions of executing these intentions. The executions of these intentions have different necessary conditions. For nothing will count as the execution of the first unless it is an operation on a circle while nothing will count as the execution of the second unless it is an operation on an angle. And this difference is perhaps enough to differentiate the two intentions. It is perhaps a sufficient condition of two intentions being different from one another that they differ with respect to the necessary conditions of their exe-cution.

Thus, it seems that it is a necessary condition of the agent's having an intention to perform a certain action, not that such an action be logically possible or that such an intention be capable of being executed, but instead that the agent does not believe that such an action is not logically possible. So the claim that an agent can intend to perform an action which is logically impossible, as long as he does not believe it to be logically impossible, seems to be true.

## 4. *Must An Agent Know What it is to do X in Order to Intend to do X?*

In this section I want to discuss another possible restriction on objects of intention. How much must an agent know about the object of the intention to do $X$ in order to be able to have that intention? For example, must he know what it is to do $X$? Is it necessary that an agent know what it is to do $X$ in order for $X$ to be a possible object of intention for that agent?

Suppose that John overhears one man say to another: 'I'd pay a very large sum of money to anyone who would build me a Sheraton sideboard.' John knows neither what a sideboard is nor what the term 'Sheraton' means. He does not even know that a piece of furniture is being talked about, nor does he know that Sheraton sideboards are made out of wood. Perhaps he also does not know what the word 'build' means. But John needs the sum of money mentioned. Can he decide to build a Sheraton sideboard and thereafter have the intention of doing so? Or can he have this intention only after he finds out what a Sheraton sideboard is?

One reason why it might be said that John does not intend to build a Sheraton sideboard is this. There is a close connection between intending to do $X$ and trying to do $X$.[1] If an agent cannot try to do $X$, it might be claimed, then he cannot intend to do $X$. And the agent cannot try to do $X$ unless he knows what it is that he is trying to do. For if he does not know what it is that he is trying to do, he cannot regard any action as a step towards doing that. He cannot even begin to go about trying to do $X$ or executing his supposed intention to do $X$. And an intention which the agent cannot even begin to carry out is not an intention at all. If this is so, then John cannot try to build a Sheraton sideboard and hence cannot intend to build a Sheraton sideboard. John has no grounds for believing that doing this rather than that will bring about the existence of a thing fitting the description 'Sheraton sideboard'.

[1] This connection will be discussed in Chapter 5.

It might be said: even if John has no grounds for believing that doing this rather than that will bring about the existence of something fitting that description, he can still try to do so. For doing $Z$ will count as trying or part of a process of trying to bring about this as long as John believes that doing $Z$ is a step in bringing this about and does $Z$ with the intention of bringing this about. But this not only begs the question by assuming that the agent does intend to build a Sheraton sideboard. It also raises the same type of question again in a somewhat different way. For it will be replied that John cannot even believe that something will bring it about that $K$ if he does not know what $K$ is. If a person does not know what '$X$' and '$\Phi$' are, he can perhaps believe that the sentence or statement '$x$ is $\Phi$' is true, but he cannot believe that $x$ is $\Phi$.

Let us suppose, then, that John cannot try to bring it about that $K$ if he knows nothing about $K$. But John does know something about what it is that he has to do in order to earn the sum of money, namely that it is *called* 'building a Sheraton sideboard'. So he can find out what is involved in building such a piece of furniture. We can speak of his consulting a dictionary and then a book on furniture styles as the first steps in his building a Sheraton sideboard (though, perhaps, not as part of his trying to build a Sheraton sideboard). What John intends to do, then, is to build something that answers to the description 'a Sheraton sideboard'. First, he can intend to do $X$ as long as he knows enough about $X$ to enable him to put himself in a position to try to do $X$. Second, he does know that he will have executed his putative intention when he has built something answering to this description. And that he knows this much makes it possible for him to have this intention. As we saw in Section 3, a necessary condition of having a certain intention is knowing what would count as the carrying out or the execution of that intention. And John fulfils this condition. Thus, if the agent knows enough at $t_1$ to be able to find out what it is to do $X$, he can at $t_1$ intend to do $X$. And he can, at a later time than $t_1$ (after he has found out what it is to do $X$), begin to try to do $X$.

An analogy may be drawn here between the situation in intending and the situation in referring. What John intends to do is to build *whatever* it is that satisfies the description a 'Sheraton sideboard' or to do *whatever* satisfies the description 'building a Sheraton sideboard'. Suppose that a drawing has just taken place for the grand prize in some raffle for charity and the chairman of the raffle committee announces the winner by saying: 'Jane Smith has won the grand prize.' Suppose further that the chairman was thereby referring to a certain person and that the chairman does not know Jane Smith – and in fact he does not know any of the properties of this person except that a ticket in the raffle was bought in this person's name. The chairman is referring to *whoever* bears the name of 'Jane Smith'. If there is one and only one such person, then the chairman is referring to that person, even if all that he knows about the person to whom he is referring is that that person is named 'Jane Smith'. In fact, if there is one and only one person in the world who bears the name 'Jane Smith', then a speaker would be referring to that person by saying, 'Jane Smith has property $\Phi$,' even apart from a special context such as a raffle. The speaker in such a case may, for example, have been told that Jane Smith has this property without being told who Jane Smith is, and he may now be giving someone else this information. The use of the *name* 'Jane Smith' is, if there is only one person having this name, sufficient by itself to make the speaker's remarks be *about* that person rather than some other person. And similarly, that John knows the *name*, so to speak, of the action in question – 'building a Sheraton sideboard' – is sufficient by itself to render his intention an intention *about* that action rather than some other action or no action at all.[1]

Thus, an agent can intend to do $X$ at $t_1$ even if he does not know at $t_1$ what it is to do $X$ or what is involved in doing $X$, although he must know something about $X$ at $t_1$.

## 5. *Compound Objects of Intention*

Suppose that an agent decides to do whatever will bring it about that $K$ and later finds that only either doing $X$ or doing $Y$ will bring this about. Before he decides which of these he will do, he can truly say that he intends to do either $X$ or $Y$. The agent also intends to do *only one* action, however. But if we say that in intending to do either $X$ or $Y$,

---

[1] There are important differences between intending and referring, however. For example, a speaker can try to refer to a certain individual and succeed in doing so. But it is not meaningful to talk about an agent's trying to intend to do $X$ and succeeding in intending to do so. The situation with respect to referring is discussed further in my *Talking About Particulars* (Routledge and Kegan Paul, 1970).

the agent intends to perform only one action, then it appears that 'either $X$ or $Y$' cannot be the object of the agent's intention. For it appears that either it is the case that 'either $X$ or $Y$' is two actions or else 'either $X$ or $Y$' is not an action at all (because a disjunction of actions is not itself an action). If 'either $X$ or $Y$' is two actions, then it cannot be the object of the agent's intention, since he intends to perform only *one* action. And if 'either $X$ or $Y$' is not an action, then it still cannot be the object of the agent's intention, since he intends to perform an *action*. Furthermore, we cannot say that in intending to do either $X$ or $Y$, the agent either intends to do $X$ or else intends to do $Y$. For this would be true only if (i) the agent intended to do $X$, or (ii) the agent intended to do $Y$, or (iii) the agent intended to do both $X$ and $Y$. And the agent does not *yet* satisfy any of these conditions since he has not *yet* decided how he will bring it about that $K$.

The agent does intend to perform one and only one action. And from the above it appears that we must say that the one and only description of this action is 'something that will bring it about that $K$'. This seems to be the only way to provide a single action to serve as the object of the agent's intention. This action is such that the agent can perform it by performing $X$ or by performing $Y$. But actions $X$ and $Y$ are each distinct from this action.

One alternative to this position is to regard 'either $X$ or $Y$' as a special type of object – a compound object which is itself an action and which consists of two possible actions. We may call such an object 'a disjunctive pair of actions'. Execution of this intention would presumably involve a performance directed at the disjunctive pair. But what can be meant by calling such an object 'an action'? And what can be meant by 'performance of a disjunctive pair'? This could only mean 'performance of one or the other or both members of that pair'. But then, when an agent performs any single action, he performs an indefinite and probably infinite number of disjunctive pairs of actions having that action as one member. Since the first alternative – that the agent intends to perform an action distinct from both $X$ and $Y$ called 'something that will bring it about that $K$' – does not involve this consequence, the first alternative seems preferable to the second. Hence we will say that in such cases as the above, only an individual action – not special objects, such as disjunctive pairs, which are apparently not actions at all – can be the object of the agent's intention.

It must be pointed out, though, that we have been dealing with a special case of disjunctive intentions – the case in which the two disjuncts are held together by a common further purpose (in our example, to bring it about that $K$). Presumably some other solution of the problem of disjunctive intentions would have to be given for those cases in which there was no such further purpose.

# PART TWO

# The Relations between Intending and Other States and Activities

# 4 Intending and deciding

## 1. *Deciding and Deliberation*

To decide to perform an action $X$ is partly to form an intention to do $X$. A necessary condition of the agent's deciding at time $t_i$ to do $X$ at time $t_j$ is that the agent not have had the intention of doing $X$ for a certain period of time prior to $t_i$. A second necessary condition of his having decided at $t_i$ to do $X$ at $t_j$ is that during a period of time after $t_i$ he intends to do $X$ at $t_j$.[1] But these necessary conditions do not together form a sufficient condition of deciding to do $X$. For an agent can come at $t_i$ to have, and can continue for a period of time to have, the intention of doing $X$ at $t_j$ without having decided to do $X$ at $t_j$. For example, when a person goes to a restaurant, he may intend to order a certain dish without having decided to do so. He may have wanted to go to that restaurant because that restaurant serves that particular dish and have therefore decided to go to that restaurant, but this is not the same as deciding to order that dish. Another example is this. A person who arrives at a railroad station and who, upon finding that there is only one more train to his destination that day, forms the intention of taking that train, does not necessarily decide to take that train. Here is a third example. A suburban commuter can intend to take a certain commuter train on a certain morning without having decided to take that train on that morning (although he may have decided to take that train on some previous morning and thereafter have taken that train every morning). What further conditions must the formation of an intention satisfy in order that that formation of an intention count as a decision?

In what follows, I will be talking about what are sometimes called the 'central cases' of deciding. These are the cases about which we have no hesitation in saying that they are cases of deciding. They are the cases which exhibit the features of deciding most clearly. There are

[1] This period of time may be quite short, as in cases in which the agent begins to perform the action in question very soon after deciding to do it.

perhaps some cases in which we would use the term 'deciding' which appear not to exhibit these features. But I believe that either we would, upon reflection, say that these are not cases of deciding or else that these cases are related to clear cases of deciding in certain definite ways.

Deciding to do $X$ seems to be closely related to deliberation. It seems that nothing can count as a decision to do $X$ unless the agent has deliberated about doing $X$. So it is possible that the three conditions consisting of: (i) the two necessary conditions of deciding to do $X$ which were mentioned in the first paragraph; (ii) the agent's having deliberated about doing $X$; (iii) the agent's having formed the intention to do $X$ *as a result of* having deliberated about doing $X$, are each a necessary condition of and together form a sufficient condition of the agent's having decided to do $X$.

But let us now consider the following case. The agent deliberates about doing $X$ but has not yet reached a decision about this; then he finds out that a factor which he formerly did not believe to be present in the situation is in fact present; upon learning that this is so, he immediately decides to do $X$. In this case, the formation of the intention to do $X$ certainly occurred after the process of deliberation took place. But did the agent form that intention as a result of deliberating about doing $X$? His forming of that intention is not a direct result of his deliberation and, further, is not a result solely of his deliberating about the matter while having certain beliefs. It seems that what directly decided the agent to do $X$ was his *coming to believe that* the new factor was in fact present in the situation, not his *deliberation about* the other factors which he believed to be present in the situation. And since the formation of this intention seems to be at least partly and directly a result of his coming to have this belief, we cannot say that he came to have this intention as a direct result solely of deliberating about doing $X$. Yet he did decide to do $X$. What this shows is that we should not interpret the phrase 'as a result of' in (iii) to mean 'as a direct and sole result of'. Certainly it is at least possible that in the case just described, his coming to have that intention is at least partly a result of his deliberating about doing $X$. For his coming to believe that the new factor was present in the situation might not have led him to decide to do $X$ unless he had already deliberated about doing $X$. For example, he may have found upon deliberation that the other factors were evenly balanced. Thus, as a result of deliberation he was in a position to know that the presence of the new factor tipped the balance in favour of doing $X$.

But although there are cases of the sort described, there are also cases in which the agent decides to do $X$ without having previously deliberated about *doing* $X$, as when he comes to believe that a new factor is present and immediately decides to do $X$. And this sort of case shows that the theory of deciding previously proposed is not satisfactory. This type of case also shows that the following view is not satisfactory. It might be said that to decide to do $X$ is to form the intention of doing $X$ after considering reasons for and against performing actions where some of the reasons considered would be cited by the agent in explaining why he intended to do $X$. This definition is better than the first definition proposed. For it could be the case that, even if the agent had previously deliberated but not about *doing* $X$ and had then immediately decided to do $X$ upon learning of the new factor, nevertheless he would cite some of the reasons which he considered during deliberation as reasons for doing $X$. But this is not necessarily so. The new factor might introduce considerations of a quite different sort – that is, of a sort about which he had not yet deliberated at all. So the case in which the agent decides to do $X$ immediately upon learning of a new factor shows that this view is not satisfactory either.

It is clearly not true to say only that to decide to do $X$ is to form the intention of doing $X$ *after* deliberation. For on this view, as soon as the agent has once deliberated about some one thing, every subsequent formation of an intention will count as a decision, even if that which the agent thereupon intends to do is completely unrelated to that one thing about which he deliberated. But agents who have previously deliberated about something thereafter form many intentions about actions unrelated to that about which they deliberated without such formations of intentions being decisions. The first position described above does not show certain cases of deciding to be cases of deciding because an agent can decide to do $X$ even when he did not deliberate about doing $X$. But the second position just proposed shows cases to be cases of deciding which are in fact not cases of deciding. This shows that in cases of deciding there is a stronger relation between the required process of deliberation and forming the intention to do $X$ than merely one of temporal succession (that is, than the relation mentioned in the second position). But the relation between

E

these two is not as strong as that mentioned in the first proposed definition.

## 2. *Alternative Actions and Deliberation*

In the previous section I said that an agent can decide to do $X$ without having deliberated about *doing* $X$. But I think that he cannot have decided to do $X$ without having deliberated about *something* which has a certain relation to doing $X$. In what follows, I want to show what this relation is.

Let us consider next the following position: to decide to do $X$ is to form the intention of doing $X$ after a process of deliberation of which $X$ is a possible object. Suppose that the agent is deliberating about what to do in a certain situation. Action $X$ is a possible object of this particular process of deliberation if and only if either (i) the agent does in fact deliberate about doing $X$ during this process (in which case $X$ is not only a possible object but also an actual object of this process of deliberation), or (ii) the agent does not deliberate about doing $X$ during this process but he could have deliberated about doing $X$ during this *same* process and have decided to do $X$ as a result of *this* process of deliberation. The application of this definition clearly requires criteria for determining what counts as a single process of deliberation or as the same process of deliberation. For example, suppose that the agent begins at time $t_4$ to deliberate about the best way to go to Europe next year. He deliberates about this up to time $t_8$, at which moment he immediately begins to deliberate about whether or not to accept a certain job and continues to deliberate about this until time $t_{12}$. Let us suppose that the agent has performed just one process of deliberation during the time $t_4$ to $t_{12}$. Then it appears that any action whatsoever will be a possible object of this process of deliberation on the above definition of 'possible object of a particular process of deliberation'. For if the agent is said to have deliberated, in one and the same process of deliberation, about two such different topics as a certain job on the one hand and modes of travel on the other, then he *could* have deliberated about any topic whatsoever in that one and the same process of, deliberation. And since he could have deliberated about any topic whatsoever in that process, any action whatsoever *could* have been intended as a result of that process of deliberation. For given any action, there is some topic to which that action is related and which could have been deliberated about in that one and the same process of deliberation. This shows that some requirement is necessary pertaining to the relation between the subject-matter or topic *which is in fact deliberated about* and the action which is to be regarded as a *possible* object of that process of deliberation. This requirement should concern subject-matter in such a way that not every *topic* could be deliberated about in one and the same process of deliberation. Such a requirement would show that there were in fact two processes of deliberation (temporally contiguous with one another) in the example described above.

This requirement can be put in terms of the notion of an action's being an *alternative* to other actions with respect to a certain topic. Thus, $X$ is a possible object of a given process of deliberation if, and only if, the agent does or would regard $X$ as an alternative to the actions about which the agent *is in fact* deliberating about with respect to the topic *being* deliberated about. What counts as an alternative is connected with the topic about which deliberation *is* taking place, not with a topic which the agent *could* deliberate about. For it is quite possible that given almost any two actions, there is a topic which the agent could deliberate about and with respect to which those two actions are alternatives. For example, let us consider the action of taking a plane to New York. With respect to the topic 'modes of travel to New York', the action of having dinner at a given restaurant is not an alternative to the action of taking a plane to New York. But with respect to a situation in which the agent wants to do either one or the other of these actions at a given time and cannot do both – as, for example, when the plane for New York leaves at exactly the time $(t_i)$ at which the restaurant opens – they are alternatives.[1] Thus, they are alternatives with respect to the topic 'doing something which the agent wants to do in this situation or at time $t_i$'. This is why practically any two actions could be alternatives: it is always possible that the agent wants to perform both actions and yet the situation is such that he can perform only one of them.[2]

---

[1] This is not to say that two actions are alternatives only when only one of them can be performed at a given time.

[2] This argument does not show that two actions each of which is necessarily inseparable from the other can be alternatives to one another. That is why I have said that *almost* any two actions could be alternatives to one another rather than saying that this is possible for *every* pair of actions.

But not every action is an alternative to a given action with respect to the topic *being* deliberated about. Because the topic which is in fact being deliberated about limits what counts as alternatives, the notion of an alternative could be used to provide a criterion of 'one and the same process of deliberation'. We can also instead use the notion of an alternative to give directly a definition of 'deciding' which does not use the term 'one and the same process of deliberation'. Here is the definition of 'deciding' in terms of this notion of an alternative: *To decide to do X is to form the intention of doing X after a process of deliberation with respect to which X is one of the alternatives which the agent considered or else with respect to the topic of which X would be regarded by the agent as an alternative to the actions that he did consider.*

## 3. *Deciding to Bring It About That K by Doing X.*

There are cases in which the agent decides to do $X$ but to which the notion of an alternative action, as so far explained, does not apply. For example, the agent may deliberate about which result to try to bring about. He may decide to bring it about that $K$ by doing action $X$. Yet $X$ is not an alternative with respect to this process of deliberation. For since the agent did not deliberate about doing $X$ itself, $X$ could be an alternative with respect to this process only if the agent did deliberate about performing an action to which $X$ is or would be regarded by the agent as an alternative. In this particular case, the actions which the agent did deliberate about performing are the actions 'bringing it about that $K$' and 'bringing it about that $L$'. $X$ is a means of bringing it about that $K$ and so is not an alternative to bringing it about that $K$. And $X$ does not seem to be an alternative to bringing it about that $L$. For the agent would not deliberate about either doing $X$ or else bringing it about that $L$. He would deliberate about bringing it about that $K$ or bringing it about that $L$, and then about doing $X$ only if he went on to deliberate about the means which he should use to bring it about that $K$. $X$ is an alternative with respect to other means of bringing it about that $K$, not with respect to what result to bring about. Hence, on our view the agent cannot have decided to do $X$. But the agent did decide to do $X$.

There are two sub-types of this type of case which must be distinguished from one another. In one sub-type, the agent already knew what the means of bringing it about that $K$ were, and in particular that doing $X$ was such a means, while he deliberated about what result to bring about. Here the action $X$ is a member of what we might call a disjunctive alternative – the disjunction of the various actions which the agent believes to be means to bringing it about that $K$. There is a sense in which the agent will do either the action 'bringing it about that $L$' or one of the actions which are means to bringing it about that $K$. These are alternatives because the agent knows that he will perform either one or the other if he decides to perform either action about which he is deliberating. And in this sense $X$ is an alternative to bringing it about that $L$: $X$ is a member of a disjunction which disjunction is regarded by the agent as an alternative to bringing it about that $L$. In such a case the agent does decide to do $X$. But in the second type of case the agent forms the intention of doing $X$ immediately upon deciding to bring it about that $K$ without having believed that doing $X$ was a means of bringing it about that $K$ while he deliberated about whether to bring it about that $K$ or to bring it about that $L$. In this case it is doubtful that we would say that he had decided to do $X$, although he now intends to do $X$.

It might be objected that on this view an action can be an alternative to itself. For in a case of the first sub-type, we can add the action 'bringing it about that $L$' to the disjunction of which $X$ is a member. And then since $X$ is an alternative to bringing it about that $L$ through being a member of this disjunction, bringing it about that $L$ would also be an alternative to bringing it about that $L$ through being a member of this disjunction. However, bringing it about that $L$ cannot be a member of this disjunction. For this disjunction has as disjuncts only actions which the agent believes to be means to bringing it about that $K$. That these disjuncts are believed to be related in this way to an alternative to bringing it about that $L$ is the reason why they themselves are alternatives to bringing it about that $L$.

## 4. Choosing

It might also be objected that there are cases in which the agent is presented with two or more alternatives and must take one of them immediately. In such a case there is no time in which the agent can deliberate, but he might still be said to have decided to take one of the alternatives rather than the other. For example, the agent is driving down a road and suddenly comes to a fork in the road; he immediately decides to take the right-hand branch rather than the left-hand branch. Cases such as these show that deliberation is not a necessary condition of deciding to do $X$.

But this is not correct. If it is in fact the case that the agent did not have time to deliberate about doing $X$ before he had to take one or the other of the alternatives, then the agent did not decide to do $X$. Instead, he merely chose to do $X$. A case of choosing may also be a case of deciding. Suppose that a person presents the agent with a deck of cards and asks the agent to choose one of them. If the agent deliberates about which card to take and then takes one of them, we can say either that he decided to take that card or that he chose that card or that he decided to choose that card. We can say any or all of these because the essential features of deciding and the essential features of choosing are both present in this case. The agent deliberated about the alternatives and then formed the intention to perform one of the actions about which he deliberated; thus, this is a case of deciding. The agent was presented with a definite set of alternatives and had to perform an act of selection which is a physical action or partly a physical action, such as saying something, pointing to something, taking a certain object, or (in the case of the fork in the road) travelling down one of the branches; thus, the case of the cards is also a case of choosing. If the agent had not deliberated about doing one of these actions, then the agent would be said merely to have chosen and not also to have decided. Merely choosing is, in the large majority of cases of merely choosing, identical with performing a (partly or wholly) physical action after being presented with a set of alternatives, or (in such cases as that of choosing a number after being asked by someone to do so) identical at least with doing more than merely forming an intention to perform a certain action if not identical with performing an action which is partly physical. Since choosing always involves more than deliberation, and merely choosing does not involve deliberation at all, deciding and choosing are quite different activities. And if, in the case of the fork in the road, the agent did not deliberate about which road to take before he took the right-hand branch, then this case is a case of merely choosing and not of deciding.

That choosing is often identical with performing a (partly or wholly) physical action is shown by the following case. Suppose that the agent knows that another person is about to request him to choose a card.

He can say: 'If that person asks me to choose a card, I intend to choose the card on that end.' But he could also say instead: 'I intend to take the card on that end.' That the agent can talk about the physical action (taking the card) instead of talking about choosing the card shows that when he performs that physical action, that physical action is identical with his choosing that card. He now intends to choose that card. But having formed the intention of taking a certain card, even after having deliberated about which card to take, is not identical with having chosen that card. Thus, this shows that deciding and choosing are quite different. It is necessary that the agent perform a (partly or wholly) physical action, which is a selection of one of the alternatives, in a case of choosing.

## 5. Deciding at $t_i$ and at $t_k$ to do X

If the agent decides at time $t_1$ to decide at time $t_4$ to do $X$, he has thereby decided to do something which he cannot do. He cannot decide at $t_4$ to do $X$ if he has already decided at $t_1$ to decide to do this at $t_4$ and has not forgotten that he has decided this or changed his mind about this between $t_1$ and $t_4$. For to decide to decide to do $X$ at $t_4$ is to decide to do $X$ at $t_4$. And the agent cannot later decide to do $X$ at $t_4$ if he has already decided to do $X$ at $t_4$, unless he has forgotten that he did so earlier or has changed his mind about doing $X$ at $t_4$. Our theory of deciding can explain why this agent cannot later decide at $t_4$ to do $X$. When the agent decided at $t_1$ to decide at $t_4$ to do $X$, he thereby decided at $t_1$ to do $X$. Thus, at $t_1$ he formed the intention of doing $X$. He cannot again form that intention at $t_4$ without having ceased to have that intention at some time between $t_1$ and $t_4$. For he cannot form a second intention to do $X$ while having the first intention. There are no conditions in which we would say that an agent has more than one intention to do $X$. This is primarily because every statement of the form 'He has an intention to do $\Phi$' must be capable of being put in the form 'He intends to do $\Phi$.' And it seems that *both* of the statements 'He has an intention to do $X$' and 'He has two intentions to do $X$' would be expressed by the one statement 'He intends to do $X$.' The form 'He intends to do $\Phi$' does not allow the application of criteria of mere numerical differences of intentions. An intention is not the sort of thing of which there can be two exactly similar but numerically different instances with respect to the same person at the same time. The statement

'He has an intention to do $X$' is synonymous with the statement 'He intends to do $X$' and allows only the sorts of differences between and among intentions with respect to one person at one time that the latter statement allows, namely differences relating solely to objects. Intentions had by one person at one time can differ only with respect to what they are intentions to do and not with respect to mere number. For differences of mere number cannot be represented by statements of the form 'At $t_1$ Jones intends to do $\Phi$', since 'At $t_1$ Jones intends to do $\Phi$ and also intends to do $\Phi$' is synonymous with 'At $t_1$ Jones intends to do $\Phi$.' Thus, the view that a decision is identical with the formation of a certain intention after deliberation can explain why the agent, having once decided to do $X$, cannot again decide to do $X$ unless he has changed his mind about doing $X$ or otherwise ceased to intend to do $X$ in the interval between the two decisions.

Could an agent have at one time two intentions to do $X$ if he had each in a different way? Let us suppose that the agent decides at $t_1$ to do $X$ and then forgets at $t_4$ that he intends to do $X$. It might be said that he still intends to do $X$ in a dispositional way. For he will intend to do $X$ in a non-dispositional way – that is, in just the way that he intended to do $X$ immediately after he decided at $t_1$ to do $X$ – if he remembers that he intended to do $X$. So at $t_6$ the agent intends (in a dispositional way) to do $X$. And at $t_6$ he can again decide to do $X$ and thereby *also* simultaneously have that intention in a non-dispositional way. It might be claimed that this is one thing that could be meant by saying that an agent has two intentions at one time to do $X$.

But this is not satisfactory either. To say that the agent intends in a dispositional way to do $X$ is to say that under certain conditions – for example, remembering that he intended to do $X$ – he would come to have that intention in a non-dispositional way. But this cannot happen in the case just described. For if by deciding at $t_6$ to do $X$, the agent does already have the intention in a non-dispositional way, then it is no longer possible for him to *come* to have that intention in a non-dispositional way. For, as we have seen, the agent cannot have two intentions to do $X$ simultaneously in a non-dispositional way. And since at $t_6$ the agent can no longer *come* to have this intention in a *non-dispositional* way because he already *has* this intention in a non-dispositional way, at $t_6$ the agent no longer has the intention to do $X$ in a *dispositional* way. Therefore, at $t_6$ the agent does not simultaneously have two intentions to do $X$.

## 6. *Deciding and Intending*

If our theory of deciding is correct, then the only step in deciding is the formation of an intention after deliberation takes place. There is no additional step named 'deciding' occurring between the deliberation and the formation of the intention which is distinct from the formation of the intention and which then brings about or results in the formation of the intention. Deciding to do $X$ is identical with the formation of an intention to do $X$ after a process of deliberation having the properties described in Section 2 has taken place.

# 5 Intending and trying

## 1. *Introduction*

Is there any intention which an agent must have in order to be correctly describable as 'trying to do X?' In particular, is intending to do *X* a necessary condition of trying to do *X*? In order to answer these questions, we must determine what it is to try to perform some action *X*.

## 2. *The Nature of 'Trying to do X'*

An agent can be correctly described as 'trying to do *X*' only if what the agent *is* doing can also be correctly described in some other way which does not involve mentioning action *X*. 'Trying to do *X*' is itself an action. For a possible answer to the question 'What is he doing?' when the agent is moving his body, is 'He is trying to do *X*.' Not only is the description 'trying to do *X*' a possible description of an action, but also, like the description 'bringing it about that *K*', the description 'trying to do *X*' is correctly applicable only to actions to which at least one other description is also correctly applicable. In order to be trying to do *X*, the agent must be doing something which is not necessarily *X*. For he can try to do *X* and possibly not succeed in doing *X*; and yet when he was *trying* to do *X*, he was *doing* something. That something, then, cannot be *X*. It must be some other action *Y*. For example, an agent can be trying to climb a mountain only if he is performing such actions as fastening ropes to spikes, moving his hands and feet in certain ways, and so on.

Moreover, there is a second necessary condition of trying to do *X*, in addition to the one just mentioned. In order to be performing the action called 'trying to do *X*', not only must the agent be performing other actions as well. It also must be the case that the agent is trying to do *X by* performing at least some of these actions, just as the agent brings it about that *K* by performing certain other actions. Let us call

66

the actions which a given agent performs while trying to do $X$ and by the performance of which he tries to do $X$ actions '$Y$'. '$Y$' thus can stand for a *set* of actions, since an agent may try to do $X$ by doing *many* different things (for example, fastening ropes to spikes, moving his hands and feet in certain ways, and so on). Moreover, two agents can be trying to perform the same action $X$ even though $Y$ in the one case is different from $Y$ in the other. Two mountain climbers may well move their hands and feet in different ways even though they are both trying to climb the same mountain.[1]

The first necessary condition of trying to do $X$ is this: The agent must perform certain other actions $Y$ while trying to do $X$. But while this condition is a necessary condition of trying to do $X$, it is not a sufficient condition of trying to do $X$. It is also, secondly, a necessary condition of the agent's trying to do $X$ that he be trying to do $X$ *by* performing these other actions $Y$. And it is a necessary and sufficient condition of the agent's trying to do $X$ *by* performing these other actions $Y$ that the agent have a certain *intention in doing* $Y$, namely, the intention of doing $X$ (and any intentions necessarily involved in intending to do $X$ such as intending to bring about certain intrinsic elements of $X$).[2] Only if this is the case will his performance of $Y$ count as his trying to do $X$. Only then will he be trying to do $X$ *by* doing $Y$. It is his having such an intention that renders his doing $Y$ 'trying to do $X$' rather than trying to do something else or nothing at all.

It is not a sufficient condition of trying to do $X$ that the agent intend to do $X$ *while* performing $Y$ rather than *in* performing $Y$. Suppose that

---

[1] A special problem arises here with respect to the lowest level of action, for example, the direct raising of one's arm. What is the other action $Y$ which a person performs when he tries directly to raise his arm? In some cases we might be willing to say that $Y$ consisted in some type of mental effort. But probably we would not be willing to say this in all such cases. And even in those in which we would be willing to say this, it may not be possible to describe this mental action independently of mentioning the raising of one's arm. We might be able to describe it only as 'trying to raise his arm'. So it is not clear that the analysis of trying which I give in this chapter will apply to actions of the lowest level. Therefore, this analysis should instead be taken as applying to the many levels of action above the lowest level.

[2] The agent may instead try to do $X$ while having the intention *to do X if he can* instead of the intention to do $X$, as we saw in Chapter 3. But, for the sake of brevity, we will speak only of the intention to do $X$ in this chapter rather than also mentioning the intention of doing $X$ if he can.

the agent intends to climb a certain mountain (and thus intends to bring it about that he arrives at the top of the mountain). As part of his preparations, he goes to another mountain of exactly the same height as the first and climbs this second mountain as practice for climbing the first mountain. Let us suppose that in the course of climbing this second mountain the agent performs exactly the same actions that he will perform in climbing the first mountain. Even though he performs these same actions *while* he has the intention of climbing the first mountain – since he is climbing the second mountain in order to become able to climb the first mountain – nevertheless he is not therefore trying to climb the first mountain when he is in the process of climbing the second mountain. For his intention *in* performing $Y$ on the second mountain is to reach the top of the second mountain, not to reach the top of the first mountain. It is necessary not only that he performs $Y$ while he has the required intention but also that the required intention be his intention *in* performing $Y$ or the intention *with which* he performs $Y$.

His intention in performing $Y$ on the second mountain, though not to reach the top of the first mountain, is nevertheless *to become able* to reach the top of the first mountain. Since the agent does intend to become able to reach the top of the first mountain, on our theory of trying it is the case that in performing $Y$ on the second mountain, the agent is *trying* to become able to climb the first mountain. And *in fact* the agent can be correctly described as trying to do this. That this is so provides support for our theory.

Thus, performing $Y$ and having the intention to do $X$ as one's intention in performing $Y$ are necessary conditions of trying to do $X$. But, it might be said, these two necessary conditions together do not, at least for some actions $X$, form a sufficient condition of trying to do $X$. Let us suppose that the agent intends to climb Mountain G. He goes to the base of Mountain H and begins to climb Mountain H, believing Mountain H to be Mountain G. Let us also suppose that in climbing Mountain H, he happens to perform just those actions which he would have performed had he been climbing Mountain G instead. And he performs these actions $Y$ with the intention of reaching the top of Mountain G. Thus, he satisfies the two necessary conditions stated above. But can what he is doing be correctly described as 'trying to climb Mountain G?' The following two statements are true: (1) the agent is trying to climb the mountain that he is now on; (2) the agent is trying to climb what he takes to be Mountain G. Why should we not consider the statement (3) 'The agent is trying to climb Mountain G' to be true as well? It seems that the only reason why we should not consider (3) to be true as well is that the agent is not doing something which, if completely performed, will result in the fulfilment or carrying out of his intention. For even if he reaches the top of the mountain on which he is climbing, he will not have climbed Mountain G. To say this, however, is to say that a necessary condition of the agent's trying to do $X$ is that he be doing something $Z$ which, if completed, will result in his carrying out the intention with which he performed $Z$. In the case being discussed, it is to say that the agent can be trying to climb Mountain G only if his performance of all of the actions involving fastening of ropes to spikes, moving his hands and feet in certain ways, and so on, will result in his carrying out of his intention of reaching the top of Mountain G – that is, will result in his reaching the top of G.

If this were a necessary condition of trying to do $X$, then the only way in which an agent could try to do $X$ and yet not succeed in doing $X$ is by not completing the series of actions $Z$ which he believes will result in the fulfilment of his intention. For on the view being considered, he could be trying to do $X$ only if he is doing something $Z$ which, if done completely, will result in his having done $X$. But this is in fact not a necessary condition of trying to do $X$. An agent may complete such a series of actions and then find out that he has not brought about that which he intended to bring about. But he still can be described as having tried to do $X$ and therefore, while he is performing the actions $Z$, as trying to do $X$. For example, an early scientist may have *completed* a series of actions which he believes would result in separating a certain mineral from its ore and then find that this process had not done this. Nevertheless, he still was trying to separate that mineral from its ore. Consequently, it is not a necessary condition of trying to do $X$ that the agent perform a series of actions $Z$ which, if completed, will in fact bring about that which the agent intends to bring about. If this is so, then the agent who is climbing on Mountain H, while believing it to be Mountain G, is trying to climb Mountain G. Thus, performing certain actions $Y$ with the intention of doing $X$ is a sufficient condition of trying to do $X$.

But then, are there any restrictions on $Y$? That is, in order to be trying to do $X$, must the agent perform one or another series of actions

69

which belong to a restricted set of series of actions, or can he perform *any* series of actions as long as his intention in performing those actions is to do $X$? It seems that the agent may perform any series of actions and still be trying to do $X$ as long as his intention in performing this series is of the required sort.

However, there is one restriction – that is, one condition which must be fulfilled – although it is not a restriction on what actions the agent may perform in trying to do $X$. The condition is this: the agent must believe that there is some probability that the performance of those actions will consist in or bring about the doing of $X$ and must be able to give some reason for his having this belief. Thus, *no* series of actions is *in itself* ruled out from being *a* $Y$ with respect to trying to do $X$. For it is likely that given any such series, there is a set of beliefs which an agent could have that make it reasonable for that agent to believe that performing that $Y$ will consist in or bring about the doing of $X$. Although performing $Y$ with the required intention is a sufficient condition of trying to do $X$, a necessary condition of the agent's having that intention *in doing* $Y$ is that the agent have the beliefs just described.

### 3. *Doing Y Intentionally When Trying to do X*

Can the agent try to do $X$ and yet unintentionally perform the $Y$ in question?

Let us suppose that a person wants to get to the airport. He picks up the phone to call a taxicab but instead dials the number of a helicopter company without realizing that he has done so. He arranges to be taken to the station, still without realizing that he has arranged for a helicopter to do so instead of a taxi. The agent tried to arrange to get to the airport and succeeded in doing so. Here the symbol '$X$' stands for 'arranging to get to the airport'. The agent tried to do this by picking up the telephone, dialling the number of a transportation company, and so on – these actions being the $Y$'s in this case. The actions which the agent performed unintentionally are 'calling a helicopter company', 'arranging to be taken by helicopter to the airport', and so on. This shows that in the course of trying to do $X$, the agent may perform unintentional actions. But there are other actions – for example, 'calling a transportation company' – which are $Y$'s also and which are in this case done intentionally. The agent can perform some $Y$'s unintentionally and still be trying to do $X$ as long as there are *other* $Y$'s which he does perform intentionally and which he believes will consist in or lead to his doing $X$.

This can be shown in another way. It seems to be the case that if $W$ is an action done unintentionally, the agent cannot do $W$ *with* a certain intention. That is, the agent does not have a certain intention *in* doing $W$. If this is so, then it cannot be the case that the agent can try to do $X$ and yet *every* $Y$ that he performs is done unintentionally. For the agent is trying to do $X$ only if he is doing some $Y$ with a certain intention. Hence if he is trying to do $X$ and if he cannot perform an unintentional action with a certain intention, he must be performing some $Y$ intentionally. Performing some $Y$ intentionally is all that is required, as far as the first necessary condition of trying to do $X$ is concerned, for his trying to do $X$.

That the agent must perform some action with a certain intention in order to be trying to do $X$ shows why the agent cannot unintentionally try to do $X$. An agent cannot perform some action *with* a certain intention without knowing that he is performing that action with that intention. Therefore his trying to do $X$ cannot be done unintentionally.

## 4. *Can An Agent Be Both Trying to do $X$ and Doing $X$ at the Same Time?*

On our view, trying to do $X$ consists in performing some $Y$ with the intention of doing $X$. Thus, whenever the agent performs some $Y$ with such an intention, he is trying to do $X$. But, it might be objected, that is not true because in some cases of this sort the agent is *doing $X$,* not *trying to do $X$.* For example, let us suppose that every morning for two months Jones (who is and is known to be an expert swimmer) swims a distance of one hundred yards to a float on a lake and then swims back again. Jones is a long-distance swimmer of great experience who only recently swam the English Channel both ways non-stop. In view of this, on a given morning Jones is correctly described as 'swimming out to the float', not as 'trying to swim out to the float'. And this is the correct description of what he is doing even though he satisfies the alleged sufficient condition of trying to do $X$, since he is doing $Y$ with the intention of doing $X$. So this alleged sufficient condition is in fact not a sufficient condition of trying to do $X$.

However, in this case, Jones is trying to swim out to the float *and,* if he reaches the float, is at the same time swimming out to the float.

Jones may well be performing both of the actions 'trying to swim out to the float' and 'swimming out to the float' at one and the same time. After all, if Jones did not succeed in reaching the float, what he is doing would be correctly describable as 'trying to swim out to the float'. What this case shows is that whether or not we would *say* of the agent that he is trying to swim out to the float depends on what we know about the characteristics and past behaviour of the agent. If we knew that the agent has swum out to the float many times before in conditions such as those now prevailing or if we knew that he is an experienced long-distance swimmer and that there are no special circumstances present in the situation, we would probably say of him that he is swimming out to the float. The agent is *both* trying to swim out to the float and, if he reaches the float, swimming out to the float. What we say about him – which of these we would say that he is doing – depends on what we consider to be his chances of reaching the float. But even after he does reach the float, it is still true that he was trying to swim to the float. Let us suppose that Jones is swimming at time $t_3$ and that he reaches the float at time $t_5$. At $t_3$ the observer may truly say of Jones, 'He is trying to swim out to the float.' After $t_5$ the observer may truly say of Jones, 'He was swimming out to the float at $t_3$.' This shows that at $t_3$ Jones *is* both trying to swim and swimming out to the float. In fact, after $t_5$ the observer could truly say, 'At $t_3$ Jones was trying to swim out to the float, and he succeeded in doing what he was then trying to do.'

Whether or not the observer would in fact *say* that Jones was trying to swim out to the float depends on the observer's beliefs about Jones and about the circumstances. But that the observer does or does not have certain beliefs is not part of what the observer says when he says that Jones is trying to do $X$. For an observer could say, 'Jones is trying to do $X$,' when Jones is performing some $Y$ with the required intention[1] and thereby make a true statement even if the observer believes that it is certain that Jones will succeed in doing $X$ when this is in fact not certain. This observer does not have the beliefs in question about Jones' chances of reaching the float. Hence if he was asserting

It is important here that Jones has a certain intention in doing what he is doing. For an agent may be prevented from doing something, say swinging his arm, without it thereby being true that he was trying to perform that action. He is trying to perform that action only if he is doing what he is doing with a certain intention.

in part that he had such beliefs when he said, 'Jones is trying to do $X$,' his statement would be false. But instead, his statement is true. Therefore, he was not in part asserting that he had these beliefs when he said, 'Jones is trying to do $X$.' That he has these beliefs may be what leads him to say, 'Jones is trying to swim out to the float,' instead of saying, 'Jones is swimming out to the float.' But he is not asserting that he has these beliefs when he says the former.

An agent can try to do $X$ and do $X$ at the same time. He can try to do $X$ and yet not do $X$. But he cannot decide to try to do $X$ without at the same time deciding to do $X$ (unless he has already at some previous time decided to do $X$). Let us suppose that the agent already intends to bring it about that $K$. He does not yet intend to do $X$, even if $K$ is the intrinsic end of $X$, since $K$ may be the intrinsic element of one or more other actions too. For example, let '$X$' be 'climbing Mountain G' and '$K$' be 'reaching the top of Mountain G'. Here the agent can intend to bring it about that $K$ without intending to do $X$ since he can also bring it about that $K$ by using a helicopter to get to the top of Mountain G. In this situation, what would count as deciding to try to do $X$? It seems that deciding to do a certain particular $Y$ because doing that $Y$ will bring it about that $K$ would count as deciding on trying to do $X$, since trying to do $X$ is doing that $Y$ (perhaps among others) with the intention of bringing about $K$. But it is also deciding to do $X$. For what the agent decides is to use a certain means to bring it about that $K$. And this is identical with deciding to do $X$. Using those means to bring it about that $K$ is to do $X$. For example, he decides to perform certain movements and use certain instruments. And in deciding to use ropes and spikes rather than a helicopter, he decides to climb the mountain rather than to take a helicopter to its summit. Thus, it seems that that which would count as deciding to try to do $X$ would also count as deciding to do $X$.

If this theory of the nature of trying is correct, it shows that intending cannot be explained in terms of trying. For example, it has been said that 'I intend to do $X$' means 'I believe that I will try to do $X$ unless I change my mind.'[1] But this latter expression means, as we have seen, 'I believe that I will do some member $Y$ of a certain set of $Y$'s with the intention of bringing it about that $K$ unless I change my mind.' Thus, this expression mentions intending and cannot be used to explain what intending is.

[1] See Chapter 9.

# 6 Intention and desire

## 1. *Prima Facie Wanting and Wanting on Balance*

An agent can want to do $X$ without intending to do $X$. For the agent may want to do $X$ because he believes that doing $X$ brings it about that $K$ and $K$ is something that he wants; and yet doing $X$ also is believed by him to bring it about that $L$ and $L$ is something that the agent wants the absence of more than he wants the presence of $K$. In such a situation, the agent might say, 'I want to do $X$ and I would do $X$ if doing $X$ did not bring it about that $L$.' Let us say that in this situation the agent wants$_1$ to do $X$. Wanting$_1$ might also be called 'Prima Facie Wanting'. The agent wants$_1$ to do $X$ when he wants to do $X$ on the basis of certain considerations but not on the basis of all of the considerations which he knows or believes ought to be taken into account when deciding whether or not to do $X$.

The agent may also want to do $X$ on the basis of all such considerations. In this case we will say that he wants$_2$ to do $X$. Wanting$_2$ may be called 'Wanting on Balance'. When it was said above that the agent can want to do $X$ without also intending to do $X$ because he may also believe that doing $X$ would bring about unwanted consequence $L$, what was meant, as the example shows, is that the agent can want$_1$ to do $X$ without intending to do $X$. The agent wants to do $X$ on the basis of the consideration that doing $X$ will bring it about that $K$. But he does not want on balance to do $X$ because he wants the absence of $L$ more than he wants the presence of $K$. So he only wants$_1$ to do $X$. Thus, this shows that he can want$_1$ to do $X$ without intending to do $X$.

## 2. *Wanting on Balance and Intending*

Can the agent also want$_2$ to do $X$ without intending to do $X$? This seems to be possible. For $X$ may be that action which the agent most wants to do at $t_i$ and yet the agent does not intend to do $X$ because he believes that it is not possible to do $X$ at $t_i$. The agent might say here, '$X$ is

74

what I really want to do; but it is not possible to do $X$ now, so I'll do $Y$ instead.' And if the agent gave this reason for not doing $X$, he would not be said to want to do $Y$ more than he wants to do $X$ just because he does $Y$ instead of $X$. The reason which he gives does not mention wanting; if it did mention wanting, we would say that he wanted to do $Y$ more than $X$. For example, in the case in which the agent wants to do $X$ because it leads to the presence of $K$ but does not do $X$ and does $Y$ instead because doing $X$ would also bring about the unwanted result $L$, we would say that he wanted to do $Y$ more than $X$ and that his want to do $Y$ is a want$_2$. For that he wants the absence of $L$ affects the degree to which he wants to do $X$. But when he says that he is not going to try to do $X$ because he believes that doing $X$ is not now possible, he does not mention any wanting (of, for example, a result of $X$) which can affect the degree to which he wants to do $X$. Hence it seems that he still wants to do $X$ as much as he did (or would have) before he came to believe that it is not possible to do $X$. And it seems that this want to do $X$ is still a want$_2$ if it was a want$_2$ before he came to believe that doing $X$ is not now possible. Yet Jones does not intend to do $X$. So the statement 'Jones wants$_2$ to do $X$' does not entail the statement 'Jones intends to do $X$.'

The agent could also want$_2$ to do $X$ in a certain situation, believe that it is possible for him to do $X$ then, and still not intend to do $X$. For he could also believe that it is his duty to do $Y$ and for that reason intend to do $Y$ instead.[1] Thus, even the statements 'Jones wants$_2$ to do $X$ at $t_i$' and 'Jones believes that it will be possible at $t_i$ for him to do $X$' do not together entail 'Jones intends to do $X$ at $t_i$.' Even the statement 'Jones wants$_2$ to do $X$, believes it to be possible for him to do $X$, and does not have some other type of motive for doing some other action $Y$ which is as strong or stronger than his want$_2$ to do $X$' does not entail the statement 'Jones intends to do $X$ at $t_i$.' For Jones may still not yet have decided to do $X$ at $t_i$.

## 3. *Similarities and Differences between Intentions and Wants*

One difference between intentions and wants is this: the agent can knowingly have conflicting wants but he cannot knowingly have conflicting intentions. That is, the agent cannot intend to do $X$ and intend

[1] It might be said here that in such cases he wants to do $Y$ because he wants to do his duty. On this point, see Chapter 9, Section 3.

not to do $X$ at the same time while knowing that the objects of his intention are $X$ and not-$X$. An agent could intend to do $X$ and intend to do not-$X$ if, for example, the action 'not-$X$' were described as '$Y$' in a language with which he was not acquainted and what he intended to do was $X$ and '$Y$'. But he could not have these intentions if he knew that action '$Y$' was identical with action not-$X$. However, the agent can knowingly want to do $X$ and want not to do $X$ at the same time. He can want to do $X$ because doing $X$ is believed to bring about wanted consequence $K$ and he can want not to do $X$ because doing $X$ is believed to bring about $L$ the absence of which he wants. Of course, when the agent both wants to do $X$ and wants not to do $X$, his two wants in this case cannot both be wants$_2$. He cannot want on balance to do $X$ and also want on balance not to do $X$. Any situation in which he takes all considerations into account and is inclined equally to do $X$ and not to do $X$ is a situation which would be described as one in which he neither wants on balance to do $X$ nor wants on balance not to do $X$. It is true that the agent could want to do $X$ on the basis of a subset of relevant considerations and want not to do $X$ on the basis of another subset of considerations; and these wants could be called 'wants$_2$' since they may result from balancing the agent's wants with respect to individual considerations in the subsets in question. Let us call these 'relative wants$_2$' since they are connected with subsets of factors. Let us call the wants which result from considering *all* of the factors believed to be relevant 'final wants$_2$'. The agent cannot knowingly want to do $X$ and want not to do $X$ where these wants are final wants$_2$. The agent also cannot knowingly intend to do $X$ and intend not to do $X$. Thus, in this respect *final* wants$_2$ are similar to intentions.

A second difference between wanting$_1$ and intending is that the former admits of degrees of strength but the latter does not seem to do so. An agent can want to do $X$ (because doing $X$ brings it about that $K$) more than he wants not to do $X$ (because doing $X$ brings it about that $L$). But it is rarely, if ever, the case that one intention is said to be stronger than another.[1] Perhaps it will be said that one intention is stronger than another intention in the following type of case: the agent

---

[1] An intention can have degrees of firmness. But we rarely, if ever, talk about one intention being more firm than another. Instead, we talk about one and the same intention becoming more firm or less firm than it was before. For this reason, as well as for the reasons in what follows, firmness of intention does not seem to be very much like strength of desire.

intends to do $X$ and intends to do $Y$; then he finds out that $X$ and $Y$ are such that he can do one or the other but not both; he goes on to do $X$. In this type of case, it may seem that the agent's intention to do $X$ was stronger than his intention to do $Y$, since he went on to do $X$. But that one intention is stronger than another, even in this type of case, is doubtful. For when the agent finds out that he cannot do both $X$ and $Y$, he must decide which of these he wants to do. And during the time he deliberates about this he cannot be said to intend to do $X$ or to intend to do $Y$. If he then decides to do $X$, he again intends to do $X$. But that he again intends to do $X$ does not show that his *previous* intending to do $X$ was stronger than his previous intending to do $Y$. For these are two different states of intending – not only because the agent has them at different times but primarily because these two states of intending are based on different sets of circumstances. That he intends to do $X$ while knowing that if he does $X$, he cannot do $Y$, does not show anything about what was the case concerning his intending to do $X$ when he believed that he could do both $X$ and $Y$. So it is doubtful that we can speak of degrees of strength in regard to intending, although we can do so in regard to wanting$_1$.

Can we speak of degrees of strength in regard to final wanting$_2$? Again it may seem that one situation in which the desire on balance to do $X$ and the desire on balance to do $Y$ can be compared is that in which the agent comes to believe that he cannot do both $X$ and $Y$. If he is then undecided about which action to perform, he cannot be said to have a final want directed towards either action, just as at the same point in the previously discussed situation the agent cannot be said to intend to do $X$ or to intend to do $Y$. He then forms a new want$_2$ based on all of the considerations about which he deliberated earlier, plus the new consideration that he cannot do both $X$ and $Y$. But, similarly, that he *now* has a want$_2$ to do $X$ does not show that his *previous* want$_2$ to do $X$ was stronger than his *previous* want$_2$ to do $Y$. Thus, intentions and *final* wants$_2$ behave similarly in this type of situation too.

It might now be said that one situation in which two final wants$_2$ can be compared as to strength is that in which the agent wants$_2$ to do $X$ and wants$_2$ to do $Y$ and believes that he can do both $X$ and $Y$ although not at the same time. Then, if he does $X$ before he does $Y$, this would show that his wanting to do $X$ was stronger than his wanting to do $Y$. But this is not so. The two final wants could still be equally strong. The agent believes that he can do both but that he cannot do both simultaneously. He believes that he must first do one and then do the other. He may have arbitrarily chosen to do $X$ before $Y$ and would have been just as happy to do $Y$ first and then do $X$,

But let us suppose that his want$_2$ to do $X$ is stronger than his want$_2$ to do $Y$. Then with respect to the moment at which he does $X$, his want$_2$ to do $Y$ is not a final want$_2$. It is only a relative want$_2$. And because his relative want$_2$ to do $X$ is stronger than his relative want$_2$ to do $Y$, it is only his want$_2$ to do $X$ that becomes his final want$_2$ with respect to the moment at which he does $X$. Thus, if his want$_2$ to do $X$ were stronger than his want$_2$ to do $Y$, this would still not be a case in which two final wants$_2$ were being compared as to strength. For the agent has only one final want$_2$, namely his want$_2$ to do $X$.

On this view, it is necessarily true that his strongest want$_2$ with respect to a given moment is his final want$_2$ with respect to that moment. It is also necessarily true that if the agent acts from a want at all, he acts from his final want$_2$ with respect to the moment in question, provided that he believes that he can perform that action. This is necessarily true because on this view it is necessarily true that he has only one final want$_2$ with respect to a given moment. If two of his wants$_2$ are equally strong with respect to a given moment, then he does not have a *final* want$_2$ with respect to that moment at all. This is not to say that all actions are actions done from wants. For, as we shall see in Chapter 9, actions can be done from duty instead. Nor is it necessarily true that if the agent acts from a want, he acts from his strongest want$_1$. For the agent may have a want$_1$ to do $X$ stemming from his want for $K$ which he believes that doing $X$ will bring about; and this want$_1$ may be stronger than any other want$_1$ to perform a particular action. But he may also have several wants$_1$ not to do $X$ stemming from his belief that doing $X$ will also bring it about that $L$ and $N$ are the case, both of which he wants the absence of. And although neither of these latter is individually stronger than his want$_1$ to do $X$, together they are stronger than the latter. (It should be mentioned that the term 'want$_1$' applies both to wants for objects and states such as $K$ and to wants to do actions which in many cases stem from the wants for objects and states.)

A third difference between wanting and intending is this: wants are satisfied whereas intentions are carried out. Moreover, 'satisfying wants' and 'carrying out intentions' are not two different expressions denoting the same things. For only what the agent *himself* does can count as the carrying out of an intention, while that which the agent does not do can count as the satisfaction of a want. For example, the agent can want Jones to be nominated for the Presidency, since the agent can hope that Jones will be nominated and the statement 'Smith hopes that $p$' entails the statement 'Smith wants it to be the case that $p$.' If Jones is nominated, then the agent's desire or want is satisfied. But the nominating of Jones is something that the convention does, not something that Jones does (as long as Jones does not control the convention to the point of being able to dictate its actions). However, the agent would not be said to have carried out his intention to bring it about that $K$ unless he had done something that led in a fairly direct way to $K$'s being the case.

## 4. *Wants as Dispositions to have Intentions*

Since an agent can have a final want$_2$ to do $X$ and yet not intend to do $X$, either because he may, for example, feel that it is his duty to perform some other action instead or because he believes that it is not possible for him to do $X$, we could perhaps regard final wants$_2$ as dispositions to have intentions: 'If the agent wants to do $X$, believes that $X$ is possible, does not have some other type of motive for doing $X$ and does not have some other type of motive for not doing $X$, then he will intend to do $X$' is perhaps what is meant by 'The agent has a final want$_2$ to do $X$.' We will discuss the question of whether *wants$_2$* can be construed as dispositions to have intentions in Chapter 9. It is clear, however, that *wanting$_1$* cannot be explained as a disposition to have intentions since wants$_1$ must be mentioned in the conditionals involved in describing the disposition. Hence, explaining wanting$_1$ in this way would involve one in a very small circle.

# 7 Other aspects of intention

## 1. *The Executing of Intentions*

If an agent intends to do $X$, under what conditions does his subsequent performance of $X$ count as his carrying out or executing his intention to do $X$? Not every subsequent performance of $X$ would count as this. For example, if the agent intends at $t_1$ to do $X$ and then changes his mind at $t_2$ about doing $X$, his performance of $X$ at $t_3$ will not be the carrying out of the intention to do $X$ which he had at $t_1$. The reason why his performance of $X$ at $t_3$ would not be the carrying out of his intention to do $X$ is that at the time at which he did $X$ he no longer had the intention to do $X$. So it seems that a necessary condition of a performance of $X$ counting as an execution of the agent's intention to do $X$ is that that performance takes place while the agent intends to do $X$. The agent must intend to do $X$ while he is doing $X$ if his performance of $X$ is to be the carrying out of that intention.

That this is a necessary condition of the agent's executing his intention is shown by the fact that there are many cases in which it must first be determined whether or not the agent had a certain intention at a specific time in order to determine whether he carried out that intention at that time. For example, suppose that the agent decides at $t_1$ to do $X$ and then at $t_3$ changes his mind about doing $X$. But at $t_5$ he forgets that he changed his mind about doing $X$ while remembering that he earlier decided to do $X$. Then he does $X$ at $t_5$. Does his doing of $X$ at $t_5$ count as the execution of an intention to do $X$? It seems that the answer to this question depends to a large extent on whether an agent intends to do $X$ at a moment after he has changed his mind about doing $X$ but believes that he has not changed his mind about doing $X$. That this is so shows that having a given intention at $t_1$ is a necessary condition of executing that intention at $t_1$.

But while this is a necessary condition of executing an intention, it is not a sufficient condition of doing so. Suppose that the agent agrees to meet John at 1.30 at a particular location. Subsequently, the agent goes to that location, believing that the time is 12.30 when it is in fact 1.30, in order to see whether some items have been delivered to that location in time for his meeting with John. Since it is in fact 1.30 and hence John is there, the agent does meet John at 1.30 at that location. He thereby acts in accordance with his intention. But he met John there unintentionally. Because he did what he did unintentionally, what he did is not the carrying out of his intention. An agent can unintentionally act *in accordance with* his intention, but he cannot unintentionally *carry out* his intention. Thus, it seems that another necessary condition of carrying out an intention to do $X$ is doing $X$ intentionally.

Moreover, it seems that the two necessary conditions described above of carrying out an intention together form a sufficient condition of carrying out an intention. If an agent has an intention to do $X$ and while having this intention does $X$ intentionally, then he is carrying out that intention.

However, there seems to be another set of conditions which together also form a sufficient condition of carrying out an intention. It is a necessary condition of the agent's carrying out an intention that he perform an action as a result of which the agent no longer has that intention. But this is by itself not a sufficient condition of carrying out an intention, as the case of meeting John at 1.30 shows. For in that case the agent did perform an action – namely, meeting John at 1.30 – as a result of which the agent no longer had that intention, and yet his performance of this action does not count as carrying out or executing his intention. Another example of this is as follows: the agent intends to do $X$; then he may perform action $Y$, as a result of which he finds that certain circumstances are different from what he had believed them to be; upon finding this out, he changes his mind about doing $X$. Here $Y$ is an action as a result of the performance of which the agent no longer has the intention of doing $X$. And yet his doing of $Y$ does not count as an execution of his intention to do $X$. Of course, in this case the agent did not even act in accordance with his intention to do $X$. But as the case of meeting John at 1.30 shows, even the agent's acting in accordance with his intention, and as a result of this his no longer having that intention, do not form a sufficient condition of his having executed his intention.

It may be said that the case of meeting John at 1.30 is not a case of the agent's executing his intention to meet John at 1.30 because the agent did not meet John at 1.30 as a result of his having the intention to do so. That is, it might be said that in order to carry out the intention to do $X$, it is not only necessary that the agent not have the intention to do $X$ after doing $X$, it is also necessary that he do $X$ as a result of having the intention to do $X$. But even this condition along with the other two (acting in accordance with his intention and, as a result of this, no longer having that intention) does not form a sufficient condition of carrying out an intention. For when the agent went to the proper location at a time which he believed to be 12.30 in order to see if the items had been delivered in time for the meeting, he did this at least partly *because* he intended to meet John at 1.30. Since the time was in fact 1.30, he went to that location at 1.30 and thus met John at 1.30 as a result of his intending to meet John at 1.30. Thus, the agent's acting in accordance with his intention, doing so as a result of having that intention, and doing so with the result that the agent no longer has that intention do not together form a sufficient condition of the agent's carrying out that intention. Yet each of these is a necessary condition of the agent's carrying out his intention.

To make this set a sufficient condition of carrying out the intention to do $X$, we cannot add the condition 'and the agent does $X$ in order to carry out or with the intention of carrying out his intention to do $X$'. First, this condition itself mentions the carrying out of an intention and thus cannot be used to explain what it is to carry out this intention. Secondly, as we saw in Section 3 of Chapter 2, it is very implausible to claim that anyone ever has such a thing as an intention to execute another intention.

But we can add to this set the condition 'and the agent believes that he is acting in accordance with his intention while he is doing so'. This condition rules out the above case of meeting John at 1.30 as a case of an agent carrying out his intention. For the agent did not believe that he was in the process of meeting John at 1.30 while he was in fact doing so. Adding this condition seems to render the above set of conditions a sufficient condition of carrying out the intention to do $X$.

Earlier we saw that the set (1a) acting in accordance with the intention to do $X$ by doing $X$, (2a) while intending to do $X$, and (3a) doing $X$ intentionally forms a sufficient condition of executing the intention to do $X$. We have just seen that the set (1a) acting in accordance with the intention, (1b) as a direct result of intending to do $X$, (2b) with the result that the agent no longer has that intention to do $X$, (3b) while the agent believes (at least at some time during his performance of $X$) that he is doing $X$, also forms a sufficient condition of his executing his intention to do $X$. Moreover, each condition in each of these two sets seems to be a necessary condition of his executing his intention to do $X$. If so, then the fulfilment of all conditions of one set implies that each condition of the other set is also fulfilled.

Thus, for example, if the agent fulfils all conditions of the first set, this implies that after doing $X$, the agent no longer has the intention of doing $X$ (this latter being a condition belonging to the second set). (He may, of course, at some later time again come to intend to do $X$.) How could the agent do $X$ intentionally, while intending to do $X$, and still intend to do $X$ after doing $X$? He could still intend to do $X$ after doing $X$ unintentionally. For he can do $X$ unintentionally and not realize that he has done $X$. And if he does not know that he has done $X$, he can still intend to do $X$. But if he does $X$ intentionally, he will either know whether he has or has not done $X$ or else he will have an intention pertaining to $X$ which is different from his intention to do $X$. If he tries to do $X$ and does not know whether or not he has succeeded in doing $X$, he will have the *conditional* intention 'To do $X$ if I did not succeed in performing $X$ by doing what I just did.' This conditional intention is different from his original intention to do $X$, regardless of whether that original intention was itself non-conditional or conditional. If the original intention was itself non-conditional, then this conditional intention is clearly different from that original intention. If the original intention was itself conditional, it was necessarily a different conditional intention from that which the agent has after doing $X$ intentionally. For suppose that the two conditional intentions are identical. Then, *before* the agent does whatever he does, he has the intention (his original intention) 'To do $X$ if I do not succeed in performing $X$ by doing what I am about to do.' But then the agent cannot possibly act in accordance with *this* intention until *after* he has first done something. But he has not yet done something of the required sort. Thus condition (1a) of the first set – namely, acting in accordance with his intention – cannot be satisfied by what he is about to do. But we are trying to determine whether each of the conditions in the first set can be fulfilled and yet the agent still have the original intention afterwards. If the two conditional intentions are identical, one of the conditions of the first set cannot be fulfilled. Hence this case does not show that conditions (1a), (2a), and (3a) can be fulfilled, and yet condition (2b) not be fulfilled, since in this case condition (1a) is not fulfilled. And if the two conditional intentions are not identical – that is, if the agent has the conditional intention 'to do $X$ if I did not succeed in doing $X$ by doing what I just did' after he acts in accordance with his original conditional intention where that original conditional intention is not identical with the one just expressed – then as a result of doing what he did, the agent no longer has that original conditional intention. Instead, he now has the conditional intention just expressed which is different from his original intention. So condition (2b) is fulfilled if the original conditional intention is not identical with this conditional intention. Thus, in each of the three types of cases, if conditions (1a), (2a), and (3a) are fulfilled, condition (2b) is also fulfilled.

Again, if the agent acts in accordance with his intention while believing that he is doing so and as a direct result of intending to do the action in question, then he is performing that action intentionally. We will see in Section 2 at what moment or moments during the performance of his action the agent must believe that he is in fact performing that action in order to be performing it intentionally.

By saying in the statement of condition (1b) that the agent does the action as a direct result of his intending to do so, the following sort of case is being ruled out as not satisfying condition (1b): the agent intends to do $X$; he does $X$; his doing of $X$ creates certain conditions; in view of these new conditions, the agent forms the intention of doing $Y$; the agent does $Y$. Here the agent might be said to do $Y$ as a result of his intending to do $X$. But his doing $Y$ is also a result of his doing $X$, and it is therefore not a direct result of his intending to do $X$ in the sense in which the term 'direct result' is being used here. Consider the following case. The agent intends to talk to Jones before a meeting which is scheduled to take place during the following week. He is walking along the street and, upon suddenly seeing Jones on the other side of the street, immediately goes across the street to talk with Jones. This case might be said to be a case in which, although the agent does what he intended to do as a result of intending to do it, his action is not a direct result of his intention. For it is also a result of his walking along that street. If he had not been walking along that street at that time, it is quite possible that he would not have seen Jones before the meeting and hence would not have performed the action of talking to Jones before the meeting. However, this case is to be included in the set of cases which satisfy condition (1b). To satisfy (1b), the action does *not* have to be a result *solely* of the intention in question. Instead, what must be the case is that the agent's doing of the action in question is *not* the result or a result of something (such as another action) which is *itself* a result of *that intention*. And the case just described satisfies this condition even if it is a result of his intending to talk with Jones before the meeting together with the action of his walking along that street at that time.

Does the satisfying of conditions (1a), (2a), and (3a) imply that condition (1b) is also satisfied? Suppose that the agent intends to do $X$ at some time (where this is taken here to mean 'at some time within a definite period of time'). At time $t_4$ he is threatened by a criminal and told to do $X$ at $t_5$. There are two possible cases here. First, let us suppose that the agent wants very strongly not to do $X$ at $t_5$. Then if he does do $X$ at $t_5$ as a result of the threat, his action will satisfy condition (3a) but it will not satisfy conditions (1a) or (2a). For in this case the agent's intention is not 'to do $X$ at some time' but instead 'to do $X$ at some time which is not $t_5$'. Hence he will not be acting in accordance with his intention if he does $X$ at $t_5$. Since this case does not satisfy (3a), it is not a case in which (1a), (2a), and (3a) are satisfied and condition (1b) is not satisfied. Second, let us suppose that the agent neither wants to do $X$ at $t_5$ nor wants not to do $X$ at $t_5$. If he does $X$ at $t_5$, his action is certainly an intentional action, for whatever reason he does $X$, and thus satisfies (3a). It also satisfies (1a) and (2a). But it might be said that the agent may have done the action at $t_5$ as a result of the threat rather than as a result of his intending to do $X$ at some time. Hence, (1a), (2a), and (3a) would be satisfied and yet (1b) might not be satisfied. However, this case seems very similar to that in which the agent met Jones on the street before the meeting. The agent's action seems to be a result of both his intention to do $X$ at some time and of the threat by the criminal. He intended to do $X$ in any case, and as a result of the threat, he did $X$ at $t_5$ rather than at some other time. But it is his doing $X$, not his doing $X$ at $t_5$, that accords with his intention. *For his intention is an intention to do $X$ at some time, not to do $X$ at $t_5$.* And *his doing $X$* can result from both the intention and the threat even if *his doing $X$ at $t_5$* rather than at some other time results *solely* from the threat. Hence, it seems that even in this case, condition (1b) is fulfilled.

Could condition (3a) be replaced by the following condition: 'The agent believes that he is doing $X$ at least at some time while he is doing $X$?' This latter condition cannot replace (3a) because, as we will see in the next section, an agent can do $X$ unintentionally even though he believes at some point during his performance of $X$ that he is doing $X$. And if the agent does $X$ unintentionally, his action cannot be an execution of his intention to do $X$.

Thus, there seem to be two sets of conditions, each set of which constitutes a sufficient condition of carrying out an intention, and each member of each set being a necessary condition of carrying out an intention.

## 2. *Performing an Action Intentionally*

Is it the case that whenever an agent performs an action while knowing that he is doing so, he performs that action intentionally? Let us suppose that the agent believes that action $X$ is inseparable from action $Y$ and that the agent wants not to do $Y$.[1] He does $Y$, however, solely because he believes $X$ – which he wants very much to do – to be inseparable from $Y$. He is doing $Y$ intentionally, even though he does not want to do $Y$; and he knows that he is doing $Y$ while he is doing it. That an agent can intentionally do $Y$ while wanting not to do it, as long as he knows that he is doing it, tends to show that the agent's knowing that he is doing $Y$ is a sufficient condition of his doing $Y$ intentionally.

One case which might seem to show that the agent's knowing that he is performing a certain action is not a sufficient condition of his performing that action intentionally is this. Let us suppose that Fred is in the act of throwing a ball. He is doing so with the intention of getting the ball to George. But as he is going through the motion of throwing the ball he realizes that the ball is going to go to John instead. So for a certain period of time while he is performing the action, he knows that he is performing that action. And yet he is not intentionally throwing the ball to John. He is throwing the ball to John inadvertently. Thus, the agent's knowing that he is doing $X$ while he is doing $X$ is not a sufficient condition of his doing $X$ intentionally.

But first, it is not necessarily the case that we would say that he did not throw the ball to John intentionally. If, at the moment (or thereafter) at which Fred realized that the ball was going to go to John, he could have prevented it from doing so – for example, by ceasing to throw the ball at that moment – then, if Fred did continue to throw the

[1] The notion of inseparability was introduced in Chapter 1.

ball and it did go to John, we would say that he intentionally threw the ball to John. If he could not cease to perform the action at or after the moment at which he came to know that the ball was going to go to John, then he did not perform the action of throwing the ball to John intentionally. The following is another case of the same sort. An agent turns on a pump, believing that after ten minutes of operation a certain tank will have been filled with a certain chemical. If someone were asked what the agent was doing when he turned on the switch of the pump, that person might reply that the agent was filling the tank with that chemical. And he is performing that action during the whole ten minutes that the machine is operating, if he is performing that action at all. Five minutes after the switch was turned on the agent comes to believe correctly that instead a different tank is being filled with quite a different chemical. Thus, he knows that he is filling the other tank with another chemical *while he is doing it*. If the agent can turn the pump off at that time but instead leaves it in operation, we would say that up to that time he was filling the other tank but not doing so intentionally, and after that time he was doing so intentionally. But if he could not turn the pump off until it had completed a full ten-minute cycle of operation (at the end of which the tank in question was filled), then we would say that no part of his filling that other tank was intentional.

These cases show that it is not a sufficient condition of the agent's doing $X$ intentionally at time $t_i$ that the agent have voluntarily begun to do $X$ at some time (identical with or earlier than $t_i$) and that the agent know at $t_i$ that he is performing $X$. For in the case in which the agent could not turn off the pump prior to or at $t_i$, both of these conditions are fulfilled and yet the agent is not filling the other tank intentionally at $t_i$. But on the other hand, it is also not necessary for the agent to be doing $X$ intentionally at $t_i$ that the agent have known that he was doing or was going to do $X$ at the time at which he first began to do $X$. For, as we have seen, he could begin doing $X$ unintentionally, then come to know that he was doing $X$ at $t_i$ and could from then on be doing $X$ intentionally (if, for example, he could have ceased doing $X$ after $t_i$).

These cases also show that we should not speak of the agent's doing or not doing $X$ intentionally, but only of his doing or not doing $X$ intentionally *at a certain time*. Statements about the intentional or unintentional performance of an action should have the form 'He was doing $\Phi$ intentionally *at* $t_i$.' For these cases show that an agent may be performing an action intentionally at one moment and not intentionally at another moment while performing the action continuously.

But the following is sufficient for the agent to be performing $X$ intentionally at $t_i$: (1) the agent knows at $t_i$ that he is performing $X$; (2) whether he continues to perform $X$ at $t_i$ is in his control. This second condition may also be put as follows: His performance of $X$ at $t_i$ is voluntary. The term 'voluntary' is being used here in a sense in which Fred's continuing to throw the ball to John is not voluntary at a given moment if he could not cease at that moment to perform that action and the agent's continuing to fill the other tank with a different chemical is not then voluntary if he could not turn off the pump until after it had completed its cycle.

However, the conditions just stated are not both necessary in order that the agent be performing $X$ intentionally at $t_i$. For the agent could begin to do $X$ at time $t_h$ (where $t_h$ is prior to $t_i$) knowing that he was doing $X$, and begin to perform this action voluntarily, and yet still be performing that action intentionally at $t_i$ even if by time $t_i$ it is not possible for the agent to cease performing that action. For example, let us suppose that the correct tank is being filled with the correct chemical and that the agent cannot turn off the machine until it has completed its cycle. Even though the agent cannot turn off the machine at $t_i$, he would nevertheless be said to be filling that tank intentionally. This shows that it is not a necessary condition of the agent's doing $X$ intentionally at $t_i$ that the agent be doing $X$ voluntarily at $t_i$.

Second, let us suppose that the agent turns on the machine at $t_h$ believing correctly that a certain tank will be filled with a certain chemical; the machine cannot be turned off until it has completed its cycle. At $t_i$ (where $t_i$ is after $t_h$) the agent comes to believe incorrectly that the machine is filling another tank with a different chemical instead. Thus, at $t_i$ the agent does not know that he is doing $X$ (filling the correct tank with the correct chemical) though he is as a matter of fact doing $X$. Yet we would still say that he is filling that tank intentionally. If this is correct, then that the agent knows at $t_i$ that he is doing $X$ at $t_i$ is not a necessary condition of his doing $X$ intentionally at $t_i$. So although (1) and (2) together form a sufficient condition of doing $X$ intentionally at $t_i$, neither (1) nor (2) is a necessary condition of doing $X$ intentionally at $t_i$.

But the following seems to be a necessary and sufficient condition of the agent's doing $X$ intentionally at $t_i$: The agent is doing $X$ intentionally at $t_i$ if and only if (i) he is doing $X$ at $t_i$ and (ii) there is at least one time identical with or prior to $t_i$ at which the agent simultaneously (a) did $X$ (or began to do $X$) voluntarily and (b) knew that he was doing $X$ at that time. As long as there is such a time prior to $t_i$, the agent is doing $X$ intentionally at $t_i$ even if he does not know at $t_i$ that he is doing $X$ and even if he is not doing $X$ voluntarily *at* $t_i$. Again, the term 'voluntary' is being used here in a way slightly different from that in which it is usually used. In the usual way in which this term is used, if the agent knowingly and by his own choice starts the machine to fill the correct tank with the correct chemical, then even if he cannot turn off the machine at a later time $t_i$, he would still be said to be filling that tank voluntarily at $t_i$. But I am using this term in such a way that he would not be doing this voluntarily at $t_i$ if he cannot turn off the machine at $t_i$.

On this view, any action which the agent does not know that he is performing at *any* moment while he is performing that action is an unintentional action. To take a case already discussed in Section 1 of this chapter, suppose that the agent promises to meet John in a certain location at 1.30 in the afternoon. Later the agent goes to that location, believing that it is 12.30 when it is in fact 1.30, in order to see if some items have been delivered to that location in time for the meeting. He arrives at the location and finds that John is there since it is the time appointed for the meeting. In this case the agent met John at 1.30 at the proper location but he did so unintentionally. He did not know that he was performing this action at any moment while he was performing it. He may have believed correctly that he would meet John at 1.30 as he had promised to do. But he did not believe that the action which he was then performing in going to that location was the action of meeting John at 1.30. Thus, the class of unintentional actions contains both actions that the agent wants to do and even intends to do, such as the one just described, and actions that the agent wants not to do.

Although the agent must at some point in doing $X$ do $X$ both knowingly and voluntarily in order to do $X$ intentionally, it is not also necessary that the agent have a motive for doing $X$ that is stronger than his motives to do other actions in order to do $X$ intentionally. Suppose that the agent is asked to pick a card and is presented several cards from which to choose. He intends to choose one or another of them and in

G

fact takes the card on the right. He did this intentionally since he did this knowing and voluntarily. But he may well have not wanted to take that particular card more strongly than he wanted to take any of the other cards. He may have believed that it did not matter which card he took and merely took one of them. He might just as well have taken any of the other cards. In this case, the agent's want to take the card on the right is not stronger than any of his other wants with respect to the other cards. He would not even say that he took the card on the right because he wanted to do so. Instead, he would say that he took that card only because he had to pick one of them and it did not matter which one he took. In this case the agent does not have a final want$_2$. He does not have a motive for picking this card rather than some other card. But his action of taking the card on the right is an intentional action.

## 3. *Intention for the Present and Intention for the Future*

Many expressions of intention pertain to the future. They often have the form 'I intend to do $X$ at $t_i$', where $t_i$ is a time in the future. Are intentions always directed at the future? Or can an agent intend to do an action while he is doing it? I want to show that an agent can and often does intend to do $X$ while he is in fact doing $X$.

Let us suppose that Jones is raising his arm. We ask an observer why Jones is raising his arm, and we are told: 'He intends to warn Smith who is standing over there on that hill.' Let us further suppose that at the same time that Jones is raising his arm, Smith sees his arm starting to go up and is thereby warned. At this same moment the observer's statement 'He intends to warn Smith' is true of Jones. So at one and the same instant Jones intends to warn Smith and is in fact warning Smith. Therefore, an agent can intend to do $X$ while he is doing $X$.

It might be replied that this case only shows that the agent can intend to do $X$ while he is doing $X$ only in cases in which $X$ is an action that the agent does *in* doing something else (as, in this case, *in* raising his arm, he is warning Smith). When $X$ is done in such a case while doing something else $Y$, to do $X$ can be the intention with which the agent does $Y$. But can the agent also intend to do $X$ while doing $X$ in cases in which the doing of $X$ is not the agent's intention in doing something else?

If the agent intends to do $X$ (where the doing of $X$ is not the agent's intention in doing something else) and does $X$ without knowing that he is doing $X$, then he would intend to do $X$ while doing $X$. But then the question is: Can there be such a case – a case, that is, in which the agent does $X$ without knowing that he is doing $X$ – where the action $X$ is not an action which the agent performs in performing some other action? And even if there is such a case, this would only show that the agent can intend to do $X$ while doing $X$ only in cases in which he does not know that he is doing $X$. It still must be proved that this can happen even when the agent knows that he is doing $X$. This can be proved in the following way. If the agent intends to do $X$, he has that intention up to the moment at which he executes or carries out that intention (unless he changes his mind about doing $X$ or ceases to have that intention in some other way). But in the case of actions having intrinsic ends, the agent has not executed his intention of such an action until he has brought about the intrinsic end of that action.[1] For the agent has not executed that intention until he has performed that action; and he has not performed that action until he has brought about that intrinsic end. Thus, when the performance of such an action takes time – as, for example, climbing a mountain does – the agent has the intention to perform that action while he is performing that action, since he has that intention up to the time at which he executes it. He has the intention of climbing the mountain while he is climbing the mountain. For he has not climbed the mountain and hence executed his intention until he reaches the top.

However, there are activities that have no intrinsic ends – for example, walking. And therefore the argument just given does not show that the agent can intend to do such an activity while he does it and knows that he is doing it. But let us suppose that an agent intends at $t_i$ to go walking and then starts walking. If the agent did not have the intention to walk while he was walking, then he must have ceased to have that intention at the moment he started to walk, since he had that intention before and up to the time at which he started to walk. Let us suppose that the agent did cease to have that intention to walk at the moment at which he started to walk. He did not change his mind about walking; nor did he come to believe that it was not possible for him to walk in that situation. Therefore, if he ceased to have that intention at the moment at which he started to walk, he must have ceased to have it

[1] The notion of an intrinsic end of an action was introduced in Chapter 3.

because he executed that intention at that moment – at the moment at which he took his first step or even at which he lifted his foot to take his first step. But how could an agent execute an intention to walk merely by doing this? If at that moment something had prevented him from walking, he would say that he had intended to walk but something prevented him from doing so. He would not say that he had done what he intended to do. Therefore, he would not have carried out or executed his intention, for the agent's doing what he intended to do is a necessary condition of his executing that intention. The only intentions that he could have executed at this moment are the intentions to start to walk, to lift his foot, and so on. Thus, the agent did not cease to have the intention to walk at this moment. In this particular case he must have had the intention to walk beyond this first moment. But beyond this first moment – or, at least, beyond the first few moments – he was walking. Therefore the agent had the intention to walk during at least some of the time he was walking.

This case shows that the agent can have the intention to walk during at least part of the time that he is walking. But it does not show that he has that intention during the whole period of time that he walks. If he did not have that intention during that whole period of time, then there would be a period during which he was walking but during which he did not intend to walk.

### 4. *Intending to do X and Intending not to do X*

Intentions can have as objects either actions alone or actions to be performed if certain circumstances obtain. But so far we have considered only intentions having these types of objects where the object involves what might be called a certain mode, namely the mode of performing. There is another sort of intention having actions as objects in which the mode is 'omitting to perform'. If John intends to do $X$, the mode of his intention is 'performing'. If John intends not to do $X$, it appears that his intention has the same object as in the first case – namely, the action $X$ – but the mode here is 'omitting to perform'. However, it might be claimed that there is no such mode as 'omitting to perform'. It might be claimed that when John says, 'I intend not to do $X$,' what he means is that he has no intention to do $X$, not that he has an intention with a special mode. Thus, we must consider whether the agent in such a case does have an intention with the action $X$ as its object.

An agent can certainly decide not to do $X$ at $t_i$. But does this decision involve or result in an intention not to do $X$, or does it instead involve or result in no intention to do $X$? One reason why we must say that it involves or results in an intention not to do $X$ is this. If we did not say this, then there would be no difference between a process of deliberation about doing $X$ in which no decision about doing $X$ was made and such a process of deliberation in which it was decided not to do $X$. For if we said that the latter resulted in no intention to do $X$, then it would be just like the former, since the former does so too. There would be no difference between the two sorts of cases. Since there is a difference between the two sorts of cases, and since the difference seems to be the presence of an intention in the second case but not in the first, we must say that there can be intentions that are intentions not to perform certain actions.

Moreover, if there were no intentions not to do $X$, then the agent could make a decision that did not involve or result in the having of an intention. But this is incompatible with the theory of deciding, presented and discussed in Chapter 4, that to decide with respect to a certain action is identical with coming to have, after a process of deliberation, an intention the object of which is that action. If this theory of deciding is correct, then since the agent can decide not to do $X$, there can be intentions not to perform certain actions. For this is the sort of intention which the agent comes to have when he makes such a decision.

One who says that there are no intentions not to perform a certain action would perhaps reply to the above in the following way. The two processes of deliberation mentioned above – that which results in no decision about $X$ and that which results in a decision not to do $X$ – are in fact alike in that neither involves or results in the agent's coming to have an intention towards $X$. These two processes differ instead in another respect. When the agent deliberates about doing $X$ and decides neither to do $X$ nor not to do $X$, he is disposed to deliberate again about doing $X$. Of course, an agent who has deliberated about doing $X$ and has decided to do $X$ or has decided not to do $X$ may also be disposed to deliberate again about doing $X$. For if he believes that a new circumstance has arisen, which he believes to be relevant to the action $X$, the agent will perhaps deliberate again about doing $X$. However, this is not the sort of disposition which is had by an agent who has deliberated about $X$ but has made no decision about whether or not to do

93

$X$. He is disposed to deliberate again about doing $X$ even if he believes that no new circumstances have arisen since he previously deliberated about doing $X$. It is a criterion of the agent's having made a decision that he is disposed to deliberate about $X$ again only if he believes that new circumstances have arisen or will arise.

But is it true that when the agent has made a decision about doing $X$, he is disposed to deliberate again about doing $X$ only if he believes that some new circumstance has arisen or will arise? The agent might decide to do $X$ and yet later deliberate again about doing $X$ because he is not certain, and was not certain when he decided to do $X$, that he ought to do $X$. For example, he may believe that he has not properly evaluated all of the factors in the situation. It will be replied, however, that to the extent to which the agent is disposed to deliberate again about doing $X$, he has not in fact decided to do $X$. He has at most made a tentative decision to do $X$. What is meant by the expression 'tentative decision'? A tentative decision may be described in the following way: the agent has decided that if he had to decide at the present moment whether or not to do $X$, he would decide, for example, to do $X$; but he has not in fact decided to do $X$ yet. If he were forced to perform either $X$ or one of the alternatives to $X$ at this moment, he would choose to perform $X$. But he has not completed his deliberations about $X$ and the alternatives. Hence he has not decided to do $X$ even though he has made a tentative decision of this sort to do $X$. So, it would be claimed, the agent would deliberate again about doing $X$ or continue to deliberate about doing $X$, but this only shows that he has not yet in fact decided to do $X$ or not to do $X$.

But there is another type of situation in which the agent has made a decision to do $X$ and yet would be disposed to deliberate again about doing $X$ even if he did not believe that some new circumstance had arisen. In this case the agent has decided to do $X$ but believes that the various factors on each side are very evenly balanced. He deliberates again about doing $X$ in order to make sure that he would still evaluate the factors in the way that he previously did. Here the agent did make a decision but is still disposed to deliberate about doing $X$. Consequently, it cannot be said that the difference between the process of deliberation that results in no decision about doing $X$ and the process of deliberation that results in a decision not to do $X$ is that in the case of the former but not in that of the latter the agent is disposed to deliberate again about doing $X$ even if he believes that no new circumstances have arisen. For there are cases, such as the one just described, in which the agent has made a decision but in which the agent is also disposed to deliberate again about doing $X$ even though he believes that no new circumstances have arisen.

What has been said also shows that the expression 'Jones has decided to do $X$' cannot be taken to mean or to stand for 'Jones has deliberated about doing $X$, and as a result of this deliberation he has acquired a disposition not to deliberate further about $X$ unless he comes to believe that a new circumstance relevant to $X$ has arisen.' The above case in which the agent regarded the factors as very evenly balanced shows that the agent can decide to do $X$ even if he does not have such a disposition.

But it might still be claimed that an intention not to do $X$ is not a fundamental or basic type of intention. For it might now be claimed that what is meant by 'Jones intends not to do $X$' is that Jones intends to perform certain other actions. On this view it is not denied that Jones has an intention. An intention not to do $X$ is an intention, on this view. So this view is quite different from that previously considered. For on the previous view it was claimed that there are no such intentions as an intention not to do $X$. On the present view, it is admitted that there are such intentions. But it is claimed that these intentions are intentions to perform certain actions. In particular, the intention not to do $X$ is identical with the intention to do whatever is required in order that the agent not do $X$. For example, suppose that Jones intends not to become the owner of a certain painting that his friend is urging him to buy. On the view being considered, to say that he intends not to become the owner of this painting means that he has a conditional intention: he intends to do such things as informing the gallery that he does not desire to buy the painting, attempting to persuade his friend not to buy it in order to give it to Jones as a present, and so on, if Jones feels that one or more of these actions is necessary in order that he not become the owner of the painting.

It is possible that Jones' intention not to become the owner of the painting is an intention of the sort just described. But it might be said that this would not show that all intentions not to do a particular action are intentions to do certain actions if necessary. For there are actions that are under the agent's immediate voluntary control. And in such cases the agent need not take any steps to ensure that he does not perform the action in question. It is only necessary that he decide not to perform it. That is, it is only necessary that he intend not to perform it. There are no actions that are required to be performed in order that the agent not perform actions of this sort.

But this does not show that there are intentions not to perform actions that are not intentions to perform certain other actions. First, an intention not to do $X$ can be an intention to do whatever is required in order not to do $X$ even if nothing is required in order that the agent not do $X$. In the case of the action that is under the agent's immediate voluntary control, no action is required in order not to perform this action. But the agent can still intend to do whatever is required not to perform this action even if no action is required for this. Thus, his intention not to do $X$ can still be an intention to do whatever is required not to do $X$. Second, the agent, in intending not to do $X$, may intend not to do $X$ involuntarily as well as voluntarily even if $X$ is under his immediate voluntary control. And there may be actions which are necessary in order that he not perform $X$ involuntarily. Third, if we express his intention as the intention to do whatever *might* be necessary, then if the agent does intend not to do $X$ involuntarily too, there will be actions that *might* be necessary to prevent this even if no action is in fact necessary for this in a given situation. So even with respect to actions under the agent's immediate voluntary control, an intention not to do such an action can be a conditional intention to do certain other actions.

Nevertheless, an intention not to do $X$ cannot be merely an intention to do certain other actions if they are believed to be necessary. For if the agent does consider actions $Y$ and $Z$ necessary in order that he not perform action $X$ and thereupon intends to perform $Y$ and $Z$, why should his intention to do $Y$ and $Z$ be regarded as an intention not to do $X$ rather than as merely an intention to do $Y$ and $Z$? His intention to do $Y$ and $Z$ can be regarded as an intention not to do $X$ only because his intention *in* doing $Y$ and $Z$ or the intention *with* which he will do $Y$ and $Z$ is 'to not do $X$'. But if he does $Y$ and $Z$ with the intention of not doing $X$, then he intends not to do $X$. For whenever an agent does $\theta$ with the intention of doing $\Phi$, he also intends to do $\Phi$. Thus the agent must have the intention not to do $X$ as well as the intention to do $Y$ and $Z$. Thus, there are intentions of the sort 'not to do $X$'.

PART THREE

# Some General Theories of Intention

# 8 Statements of intention and predictions

## 1. Introduction

Before turning to some general theories of intention I want to discuss a view which is not a theory of intention but instead a general theory of statements of intention. This is the view that a statement of intention is either wholly or partly a prediction concerning the agent's future actions.[1] I think that we can learn some important things about both statements of intention and intentions themselves through discussing this view. By the phrase 'statement of intention' I mean a statement that expresses an intention. Since intentions are very often expressed by statements of the form 'I intend . . .', let us consider whether statements of this form are wholly or partly predictions.

## 2. Statements of Intention as Categorical Predictions

First, statements of the form 'I intend . . .' are either true or false. If Jones tells someone that he intends to do $X$ and he does in fact intend to do $X$, then his statement of intention is true; if he does not intend to do $X$, his statement of intention is false. Now let us consider a typical case of a categorical or non-conditional prediction, namely the weatherman saying, 'it will be fair tomorrow'.[2] Is this statement true or false, or is it neither of these? (i) Another weatherman could say, 'That's not true; it's going to rain tomorrow.' And that this can be said provides grounds for regarding such predictions as either true or false. (ii) But such predictions could also be regarded as neither true nor false for these reasons: (a) predictions are never called true or false; they are regarded as being either accurate or inaccurate; (b) if it is fair on the

---

[1] The view that 'expressions of purpose' are predictions is put forward, for example, by K. Rankin in *Choice and Chance* (Blackwell, 1961), p. 79, though he does say that they are predictions 'of a very curious kind'.
[2] An example of a conditional prediction is 'If that cloud formation moves in that direction, then it will be fair tomorrow.'

day in question, what we would say is not 'What the first weather-man said was true' but instead 'What the first weatherman said turned out to be true'; this latter implies that what he said was not true until the day came or until the fairness of that day occurred; but then what he said cannot be true as a prediction because it is not true until what has been predicted occurs, and then what is true is not a prediction but instead a statement about the present. However, it can be replied that what is meant by saying that what the first weatherman said turned out to be correct is: 'As it turned out, the first weatherman was right.' And this implies that the weatherman was right all along – hence what he said was true all along – but that it was just found out that he was right about the day's weather.

Thus, there are some grounds for saying that categorical predictions are true or false and also some grounds for saying that categorical predictions are neither true nor false. However, in either case – whether they are true or false or neither true nor false – statements of intention of the form 'I intend . . .' are not categorical predictions. First, let us suppose that predictions are neither true nor false. Then statements of intention are not predictions because statements of intention are true or false. Next, let us suppose that predictions are either true or false. A categorical prediction is false if, and only if, the event or state of affairs predicted does not take place or come to be the case. A categorical prediction can be falsified only by a future occurrence or non-occurrence and is falsified by such an occurrence or non-occurrence. But a statement of the form 'I intend to do $X$ at $t_4$' is not falsified by a future occurrence or non-occurrence. If one person says of another, 'He will do $X$ at $t_4$,' and thereby predicts what the other will do at $t_4$, his statement is false if, and only if, that other person does not do $X$ at $t_4$. But even if the agent does not do $X$ at $t_4$, his statement 'I intend to do $X$ at $t_4$' made at $t_1$ may still be true. For example, if at $t_3$ the agent changes his mind about doing $X$ at $t_4$, he still intended at $t_1$ to do $X$ at $t_4$ even if he does not do $X$ at $t_4$. In fact, he *must* have previously intended to do $X$ at $t_4$ in order to be correctly said to have changed his mind about doing $X$ at $t_4$. Because statements of intention and predictions are falsified in different ways, statements of intention are not predictions.

Categorical predictions are wholly about future occurrences. When the weatherman says that it will be fair tomorrow, what he says is not *about* something present at the time at which he makes the prediction, although his prediction is usually based on something present at that time. The statement of intention 'I intend to do $X$ at $t_4$' is perhaps at least partly about a future possible occurrence, namely the agent's performance of $X$ at $t_4$. But that this statement of intention is not falsified by the non-performance of $X$ at $t_4$ by the agent shows that this statement is, unlike the corresponding prediction 'I will do $X$ at $t_4$', not wholly, if at all, about that possible future occurrence.

It might be objected that it is not true that statements of intention are at least partly about what is the case at the time at which they are made. For the conditions which falsify such statements do pertain entirely to the future. If between $t_1$ and $t_4$ the agent does not change his mind about doing $X$ at $t_4$, forget that he decided to do $X$ at $t_4$, or cease to intend to do $X$ at $t_4$ in some other way, and yet does not do $X$ at $t_4$, then his statement made at $t_1$ that he intends to do $X$ at $t_4$, is false. And all of these conditions – changing his mind about doing $X$ at $t_4$, forgetting that he decided to do $X$ at $t_4$, and so on – are events or states of affairs which, if they occur or come to be at all, do so between $t_1$ and $t_4$. Thus, they are possible occurrences or states of affairs which are *future* with respect to $t_1$, that is, to the time at which the statement of intention is made. The set of conditions 'not changing his mind about doing $X$ at $t_4$, and so on' plus the non-performance of $X$ at $t_4$ falsifies the statement 'I intend to do $X$ at $t_4$.' And all of these are future, in the way just indicated, with respect to $t_1$. Therefore, if the fact that the falsifying condition of a categorical prediction is future with respect to the time at which that prediction is made shows that the prediction is wholly about the future, then the same fact (just described) about statements of intention shows that statements of intention are wholly about the future too and not at all about something which is present at the times at which the statements are made.

But this objection is not well taken. One of the alleged falsifying conditions is that the agent not change his mind about doing $X$ at $t_4$ between $t_1$ and $t_4$. But for the agent to satisfy this condition is for the agent to remain in the same state that he was in at the time at which he made the statement of intention. Thus, for the agent to satisfy this condition, the agent must have been in a certain state at $t_1$ which then does not change between $t_1$ and $t_4$. That is, something must have been the case at $t_1$ or at the time at which the agent expressed his intention. But the falsifying condition of a categorical prediction is not related in this way to anything that is the case at the time at which the agent makes that prediction. Hence, statements of intention and categorical predictions still differ in at least this way. Thus, statements of intention may still be at least partly about that which is the case at the time at which those statements are made.

Second, even if both statements of intention and categorical predictions are falsified solely by future occurrences and non-occurrences, statements of intention are still not categorical predictions. This is so not only because statements of intention are about something that is the case when they are made while predictions are not at all about what is the case when they are made. It is also true because categorical predictions are falsified solely by the occurrence or non-occurrence of what is *mentioned* in the prediction while statements of intention are not falsified solely by the occurrence or non-occurrence of the possible future action or omission that is *mentioned* in the statement of intention in question. This difference shows *by itself* that a statement of intention is not a categorical prediction in the way in which, for example, the statement made by uttering the sentence 'I will do $X$ at $t_4$' might be a categorical prediction or the way in which 'It will be fair tomorrow' is a categorical prediction.

### 3. *Statements of Intention as Conditional Predictions*

But it might now be objected that there are other sorts of predictions besides the sort exemplified by 'It will be fair tomorrow' and that statements of intention may be predictions of one of these other types. Second, it might be objected that the statement 'I intend to do $X$' is identical with a statement which does explicitly mention all of the conditions which would figure in a state of affairs rendering that statement false. I have said that when the agent states his intention, he does not mention, for example, the non-occurrence of his not changing his mind about doing $X$. But the objector would claim that such statements are identical with statements in which such occurrences and non-occurrences are explicitly mentioned. Then there would be no difference between statements of intention and predictions with respect to their *mentioning* or not mentioning conditions which play a role in their falsification. These two objections can be put in the following way. It might be claimed that the statement of intention 'I intend to do $X$ at $t_4$' is identical with 'I intend to do $X$ at $t_4$ unless I change my mind about doing $X$ at $t_4$ or forget that I have decided to do $X$ at $t_4$, and so on.' This latter statement does mention events the occurrence or non-occurrence of which bears on the falsification of the statement 'I intend to do $X$ at $t_4$.' And if it is then said that this latter statement is not a prediction because it is a conditional statement, it can be replied that there can be predictions which have a conditional form. For example, the weatherman might say: 'If the cloud formation continues at that speed in that direction, it will be fair tomorrow.' This may be called a 'conditional prediction'. Instead of predicting categorically or without qualification that $K$ will occur, the speaker predicts that $K$ will occur if $L$ occurs. Since the statement 'I intend to do $X$ at $t_4$' is, on this view, identical with the statement ($\Phi$) 'I intend to do $X$ at $t_4$ unless I change my mind about doing $X$ at $t_4$, and so on,' and since this latter is identical with ($\theta$) 'If I do not change my mind about doing $X$ at $t_4$, and so on, I intend to do $X$ at $t_4$', the original statement of intention has a conditional form as its logical form and may therefore be a conditional prediction. Thus, on this view a statement of intention is a conditional prediction which does mention the conditions involved in any situation in which that statement is false.

One difficulty with this position is that the original statement of intention 'I intend to do $X$ at $t_4$' is not identical with statement $\theta$. Statement $\theta$ makes it appear that the agent's not changing his mind about doing $X$ at $t_4$ is, at the time at which the statement is made, a condition of his *intending* to do $X$ at $t_4$. For $\theta$ is of the form 'If such-and-such, then I intend to do $X$ at $t_4$.' But instead this condition is in fact a condition of his *doing* $X$ at $t_4$ in the sense that if the agent changes his mind about doing $X$ at $t_4$, it is likely that he will not do $X$ at $t_4$. The agent must already intend to do $X$ at $t_4$ in order for it even to be possible for him to change his mind later about doing $X$ at $t_4$.

Of course, the agent's not changing his mind after $t_1$ about doing $X$ at $t_4$ is as much a condition of his continuing after $t_1$ to intend to do $X$ at $t_4$ as it is of his doing $X$ at $t_4$. And perhaps it is this that statement $\theta$ expresses. That is, statement $\theta$ expresses the conditions of the agent's continuing after $t_1$ to intend to do $X$ at $t_4$. However, one of the conditions of the agent's continuing after $t_1$ to intend to do $X$ at $t_4$ is that he intends at $t_1$ to do $X$ at $t_4$. So if $\theta$ is to express the conditions of the agent's continuing after $t_1$ to intend to do $X$ at $t_4$, the statement 'I intend at $t_1$ to do $X$ at $t_4$' must be included in the antecedent of $\theta$. But if this statement must be included in the antecedent of $\theta$, then $\theta$ cannot be identical with that statement or represent the meaning of

103

that statement. For knowing what $\theta$ means would then depend on first knowing what that statement means. Consequently, the statement 'I intend to do $X$ at $t_4$' is not a conditional prediction of this type.

Rather than being said to be identical with statement $\theta$ statement $\Phi$ may perhaps instead be said to be identical with statement $(W)$ 'I intend that if I do not change my mind about doing $X$ at $t_4$, and so on, I will do $X$ at $t_4$.' But if $\Phi$ is identical with $(W)$ and if $\Phi$ is also identical with 'I intend to do $X$ at $t_4$', then 'I intend to do $X$ at $t_4$' is also identical with $(W)$. But then 'I intend to do $X$ at $t_4$' is not a conditional statement, since $(W)$ is not a conditional statement. And if 'I intend to do $X$ at $t_4$' is not a conditional statement, it is not a conditional prediction.

It might be replied to this that the statement 'I predict that if $C$ occurs, then $G$ will occur' is a conditional prediction even though it does not have a conditional form. This shows that statements such as $(W)$ 'I intend that if I do not change my mind about doing $X$ at $t_4$, and so on, then I will do $X$ at $t_4$' can be conditional predictions even if they do not have conditional form.

But one can make exactly the same prediction in each possible situation by making either the statement 'I predict that if $C$ occurs, then $G$ will occur' or the statement 'If $C$ occurs, then $G$ will occur.' Thus, if statement $(W)$ is in fact a prediction, the agent should be able to make exactly the same statement as $(W)$ by making statement $(V)$ 'If I do not change my mind about doing $X$ at $t_4$, and so on, then I will do $X$ at $t_4$', where 'and so on' refers to the other ways in which the agent may cease to intend to do $X$ at $t_4$, and to the agent's being prevented from doing $X$.

First, let us suppose that $(V)$ is made when the agent does not intend to do $X$ at $t_4$ and knows that he does not intend to do $X$ at $t_4$. If 'I intend to do $X$ at $t_4$' were a prediction and were identical with $(V)$, then for the agent to make this statement when the agent in fact does not intend to do $X$ at $t_4$ and knows that he does not intend to do $X$ is for him to make a prediction similar to the following: the weatherman says, 'If the cloud formation which is now over the western part of the state continues on that course, then it will be fair tomorrow'; but the weatherman believes that there is in fact no cloud formation over the western part of the state now. If what the weatherman says in these circumstances is a statement at all, it can be only a categorical prediction – that is, the prediction 'It will be fair tomorrow.' For the weatherman must also believe that it is impossible for that cloud formation either to continue on that course or to change its course, since he believes that there is no such cloud formation. And so what the weatherman said in the antecedent does not state what he believes to be a condition of its being fair tomorrow. Let us suppose that there is a cloud formation over the western part of the state. And let us further suppose that the weatherman's statement is true, that is, that if the cloud formation continues on its present course, it will be fair tomorrow. Even so, the weatherman's making this statement does not constitute his making a conditional prediction. His linguistic act is one of making a true statement but not one of making a conditional prediction.

In this example, the antecedent of the putative conditional prediction does not state what the agent believes to be a condition of the occurrence or state mentioned in the consequent because he believes that what is mentioned in the antecedent does not exist. *The agent must believe that what is mentioned in the antecedent is a condition of what is mentioned in the consequent in order for his statement to be a conditional prediction.* An example of a different type is this: if the agent were to say, 'If the nations of Africa form a tariff union, then the weather will be fair tomorrow,' we would try to determine whether he believed that there is some connection between the economic affairs of Africa and the weather before we regarded this statement as a conditional prediction.

Now let us turn to statement $(V)$. If the agent understands what the antecedent and the consequent of $(V)$ mean, then he can believe that there is a connection between what is mentioned in the antecedent and what is mentioned in the consequent only if he believes that he intends to do $X$ at $t_4$. For only if he intends to do $X$ at $t_4$ can he either change his mind about doing $X$ at $t_4$ or not change his mind about doing $X$ at $t_4$. What could he mean by saying both that the antecedent of statement $(V)$ does state a condition of his doing $X$ at $t_4$ and yet that he does not believe that he intends to do $X$ at $t_4$? This could only show that he does not understand the expressions 'intend to do $X$ at $t_4$' and 'change his mind about doing $X$ at $t_4$', in which case it is doubtful that he would be making a prediction by making statement $(V)$. Thus, for the agent to be making a conditional prediction by making statement $(V)$, the agent must believe that he intends to do $X$ at $t_4$. But on the theory being discussed, it follows that for the agent to be making a conditional prediction by making $(V)$, the agent must believe that $(V)$ is true. For he must believe that the statement 'I

H

intend to do $X$ at $t_4$' is true and according to this theory this statement is identical with ($V$).

It may in fact be the case that for a speaker to make a statement and thereby make a conditional prediction, he must believe that statement to be true. But what was said above shows not only this. It also shows that for the agent to believe that there is a connection of the proper sort between what is mentioned in the antecedent and what is mentioned in the consequent of ($V$), the agent must believe that ($V$) is true. So if ($V$) is a conditional prediction, it is quite unlike typical examples of conditional predictions. A weatherman believes that his prediction is true because he believes that there is a connection between cloud formations and tomorrow's weather. But if the situation were the same in the weatherman's case as, on the theory being discussed, it is in the intention case, then we would have to say that the converse is true – namely that the weatherman believed that there was a connection between cloud formations and tomorrow's weather because he believed that his prediction is correct. For in the intention case – that is, the case of statement ($V$) – if it were true that statement ($V$) was identical with the statement 'I intend to do $X$ at $t_4$', then the agent would believe that there is a connection between what is mentioned in the antecedent and what is mentioned in the consequent of ($V$) because he believes that the statement 'I intend to do $X$ at $t_4$' is true and hence believes that ($V$) is true. This would render ($V$) very unlike typical conditional predictions. It is not that the agent in the case of ($V$) could not fulfil the necessary condition of his statement's being a conditional prediction (namely believing that there is a connection between what is mentioned in the antecedent and what is mentioned in the consequent). Instead, he fulfils it but does so in a way quite different from that in which it is fulfilled in typical cases of conditional predictions. For if the theory being discussed is correct, the agent fulfils this necessary condition of his statement's being a conditional prediction merely by believing his statement ($V$) to be true. But typically when a person predicts that $C$ will occur if $G$ occurs, he does so on the basis of a belief about the connection between $C$ and $G$ which is itself based on something other than his belief in the truth of his prediction.

Thus, the statement 'I intend to do $X$ at $t_4$' is not identical with either $\theta$ or ($V$). Perhaps, then, 'I intend to do $X$ at $t_4$' is identical with statement ($U$) 'If $R$ does not occur, then I will do $X$ at $t_4$', where '$R$' stands for all of the external circumstances which he believes would either lead the agent to change his mind about doing $X$ at $t_4$ or else would prevent him from doing $X$ at $t_4$. $(U)$ itself does not mention the possibility of the agent's changing his mind about doing $X$ at $t_4$ and so, it might be claimed, $(U)$ does not presuppose the truth of another statement about the agent's intending at $t_1$ to do $X$ at $t_4$ or require the addition of such a statement to its antecedent as $\theta$ did. And since $(U)$ is of conditional form, this would show that 'I intend to do $X$ at $t_4$' may be a conditional prediction.

First, $R$ will probably not be a list of all of the circumstances which would lead the agent to change his mind about doing $X$ at $t_4$ or would prevent him from doing $X$ at $t_4$. For it is very likely that the agent does not know at $t_1$ what all of these circumstances are. So it is possible that $R$ not occur and yet the agent not do $X$ at $t_4$ because some circumstances not included in $R$ did occur and led to the agent's not doing $X$ at $t_4$. And if this happens, the agent's original statement 'I intend to do $X$ at $t_4$' is not thereby rendered false. It could very well have been true and yet the agent did not do $X$ at $t_4$ because he changed his mind about doing $X$ at $t_4$ due to a circumstance not included in $R$. But $(U)$ would be false in this case. For $(U)$ is false if $R$ does not occur and yet the agent does not do $X$ at $t_4$. Therefore, the original statement and a statement $(U)$ in which $R$ is not complete would not be identical because they have different truth conditions.

Let us now suppose that $R$ is in fact complete. That is, let us suppose that the agent lists, at the time at which he expresses his intention, every circumstance which would lead him to change his mind about doing $X$ at $t_4$ or would prevent him from doing $X$ at $t_4$. But the agent can list these at that time only in so far as these belong to $R$ at the time at which he expresses his intention. Let us again call this time '$t_1$'. At $t_1$ he lists certain circumstances as belonging to $R$. He cannot list every circumstance that would belong to $R$ in every possible situation, for almost any circumstance could do so in the proper situation. So what he would list at $t_1$, if $R$ is to be complete at $t_1$, are those circumstances which, given the situation at $t_1$ and the situations which he expects to prevail at $t_2$, $t_3$, and $t_4$, he believes (at $t_1$) would lead him to change his mind about doing $X$ at $t_4$ or which would prevent him from doing so. But it is possible that between $t_1$ and $t_4$, different circumstances from those listed in $R$ would come to have these properties. For example, the agent may change his mind about the values to be attributed to various results and ends, even though the situations continue to be as he expected them to be between $t_1$ and $t_4$. Let us suppose that circumstance $G$ comes at $t_2$ to be such that if it is present, the agent will change his mind about doing $X$ at $t_4$. $G$ is not listed in $R$ because $G$ did not have this property at $t_1$ when the agent expressed his intention. And let us suppose that $G$ is present at $t_3$. The agent changes his mind about doing $X$ at $t_4$ due to the presence of $G$. He does not do $X$ at $t_4$. Thus, none of $R$ has occurred and yet the agent did not do $X$ at $t_4$. Thus, the statement 'If $R$ does not occur, I will do $X$ at $t_4$' is false. But the original statement of intention is not false in this situation. Therefore, the original statement is not identical with the conditional statement 'If $R$ does not occur, I will do $X$ at $t_4$.'

It might be objected that what this shows is only that the clause 'and if I do not change my mind about the values to be attributed to various results and ends' must be added to the antecedent of $(U)$. But there is as much justification for adding clauses describing possible situations in which the agent might change his mind about doing $X$ as there is for adding this clause about possible changes in evaluation of results (and hence the agent's possibly changing his mind about doing $X$). But then the antecedent of $(U)$ would contain a very large number of clauses. And it is highly implausible to maintain that when an agent says, 'I intend to do $X$ at $t_4$,' he is making a statement which is identical with a statement $(U)$ whose antecedent contains an incredibly large number of clauses. Yet unless all of these clauses are included, the statement of intention can be true while $(U)$ is false.

It might now be said that even if statement $(U)$ is not identical with the statement 'I intend to do $X$ at $t_4$', perhaps the statement 'I intend that if $R$ does not occur, then I will do $X$ at $t_4$' is identical with the latter. But this cannot be so. First, the objections which were raised against the claim that statement $(U)$ is identical with 'I intend to do $X$ at $t_4$' are also objections to the claim that the latter is identical with 'I intend that if $R$ does not occur, then I will do $X$ at $t_4$.' Second, the statement 'I intend that if $R$ does not occur, then I will do $X$ at $t_4$' is not a conditional statement and hence is not a conditional prediction. So even if it were identical with 'I intend to do $X$ at $t_4$' this would not show the latter to be a conditional prediction.

## 4. *Expressing Intentions and Making Predictions at the Same Time*

Could 'I intend to do $X$ at $t_4$' be identical with the statement 'I will do

$X$ at $t_4$' or 'I am going to try to do $X$ at $t_4$'? These latter statements are often made in situations in which it would be appropriate to make the statement 'I intend to do $X$ at $t_4$.' In fact these statements are often made in place of statements of the form 'I intend . . .'. And these statements seem to be predictions. So if 'I intend to do $X$ at $t_4$' were identical with statements of the form 'I will do . . .' or 'I am going to try to . . .', then this would provide some grounds for saying that the former was a prediction.

But we have already seen that statements of the form[1] 'I intend . . .' have truth conditions different from those of predictions. Thus, if the other two types of statements in question are predictions, it follows that statements of the form 'I intend . . .' cannot be identical with such statements. The statement 'I will do $X$ at $t_4$' can be a prediction. The agent may make such a statement solely on the basis of his past behaviour in situations similar to that which he expects to exist at $t_4$, in which case his statement is a prediction. The statement 'I will do $X$ at $t_4$' can also be a statement of intention; the agent can make the same statement by uttering these words instead of uttering the words 'I intend to do $X$ at $t_4$.' But when the agent is expressing an intention by uttering the words 'I will do $X$ at $t_4$,' he is not making a prediction; and when he is predicting by uttering these words, he is not expressing an intention. Could it be justifiably said that he could still be *both* expressing an intention and making a prediction by uttering these words, on the grounds that what the agent said could be taken simultaneously in both ways? It may be possible for the agent simultaneously both to express his intention and to predict what he will do by uttering these words. But in such cases we must say that the agent is making two different statements by uttering one group of words. For the truth conditions of his expression of intention are different from those of his prediction. Thus, even if the agent can do both of these simultaneously this would not show that statements of intention are predictions. It would not show that what the agent was saying when he expressed his intention was identical with what he was saying when he predicted his future behaviour. It would only show that an agent can say two different things by uttering one group of words.

It seems that the agent will use the words 'I will do $X$ at $t_4$' to express his intention when he is fairly sure that nothing will lead him to

---

[1] The expression 'statement of the form' means 'statement made by using a sentence of the form'.

change his mind about this or will prevent him from doing this. He will use the words 'I am going to try to do $X$ at $t_4$' to express his intention when he has some reason to believe that he will not do $X$ or even is fairly sure that he will not do $X$ at $t_4$. And he may use the words 'I intend to do $X$ at $t_4$' to express his intention in either of these situations and in all other situations.

Statements of intention are not falsified by the agent's not performing the action in question, as categorical predictions of future behaviour are. But we cannot define the term 'statement of intention' as 'statement about a future action that is not falsified by the non-performance of that action'. For probabilistic statements about future actions, such as 'I will probably do $X$ at $t_4$', also satisfy this description and yet are not statements of intention. That these probabilistic statements are not statements of intention is shown by the fact that an agent can say 'I intend to do $X$ at $t_4$' and thereby say what he believes to be true even though he believes that it is not probable that he will do $X$ at $t_4$. That the agent intends to do $X$ does not entail that the agent believes that he will do $X$ or that he believes that it is probable that he will do $X$. For he can, for example, intend to do $X$ at $t_4$ unconditionally and at the same time believe that it is likely that circumstances will arise which will lead him to change his mind about doing $X$ at $t_4$, although he does not now know what those circumstances might be. But the agent cannot say 'I will probably do $X$ at $t_4$' and thereby say what he believes to be true and at the same time believe that it is probable that he will not do $X$ at $t_4$. Thus, the statements 'I intend to do $X$ at $t_4$' and 'I will probably do $X$ at $t_4$' are not identical with one another.

## 5. *Statements of Intention as Partly Predictive and Partly Non-Predictive*

Although, as we have seen, statements of intention are not predictions, they may be compound statements one of the parts of which is a prediction. Could the statement 'I intend to do $X$ at $t_4$' be synonymous with one of the following compound statements?

(*H*) I am now in a certain state called 'intending to do $X$ at $t_4$' and I will do $X$ at $t_4$.

(*N*) I am now in a certain state called 'intending to do $X$ at $t_4$' and I will probably do $X$ at $t_4$.

(Q)  I am now in a certain state called 'intending to do $X$ at $t_4$' and if $R$ does not occur, I will do $X$ at $t_4$.

(T)  I am now in a certain state called 'intending to do $X$ at $t_4$' and if I do not change my mind about doing $X$ at $t_4$ between now and $t_4$, am not prevented from doing $X$ at $t_4$, and so on, I will do $X$ at $t_4$.

The statement 'I intend to do $X$ at $t_4$' cannot be synonymous with either $(H)$ or $(Q)$. For the second conjuncts of $(H)$ and $(Q)$, and hence statements $(H)$ and $(Q)$ themselves, are false in situations in which the statement 'I intend to do $X$ at $t_4$' is not false, as we have already seen. Moreover, this statement cannot be identical with $(N)$. For the agent cannot make the statement $(N)$ and thereby say what he believes to be true if he believes that he will probably not do $X$ at $t_4$, but he can do this while having this belief by making the statement 'I intend to do $X$ at $t_4$.' It might be objected that if the agent does believe that it is not probable that he will do $X$ at $t_4$, what he intends is not to do $X$ at $t_4$ but instead to try to do $X$ at $t_4$. But how can the agent intend to try to do $X$ at $t_4$ without also intending to do $X$ at $t_4$? As we saw in Chapter 5, the agent cannot try to do $X$ without intending to do $X$. His having a certain intention is what renders what he does 'trying to do $X$' instead of 'trying to do $Y$' or merely 'doing $Z$' (where $Z$ is what he does in trying to do $X$ or what he is trying to do $X$ by doing). And his having this intention together with his intention to do $Z$ is identical with his intending to do $X$.

Could the statement 'I intend to do $X$ at $t_4$' be synonymous with statement $(T)$? The second conjunct of statement $(T)$ is supposedly a conditional prediction. This second conjunct is in fact statement $(V)$ which we discussed previously. And the same argument that was given with respect to $(V)$ can be given with respect to $(T)$. The second conjunct of $(T)$ will be a conditional prediction only if the agent believes that $(T)$, and hence believes that the second conjunct of $(T)$ is true. Therefore, the statement 'I intend to do $X$ at $t_4$' cannot be synonymous with statement $(T)$.

Thus, statements of intention are not predictions, either in whole or in part.

# 9 Intentions as beliefs and as sets of wants and beliefs

## 1. *Intentions as Beliefs*

In this chapter I consider two views of what intentions are, namely beliefs on the one hand and sets of wants and beliefs on the other.

The first position to be discussed is that to intend to do $X$ is to believe that one will try to do $X$. This position has been put forward by Hampshire and Hart. They say ' . . . the minimum force of "I intend to do $X$" is "I believe that I will try to do X",' when certain qualifications are taken into account.[1] Thus, they seem to hold that to intend to do $X$ is, at least in part, to believe that one will try to do $X$ with certain qualifications, since they seem to say that to express such an intention is, at least, to express a belief. The qualifications which they mention concern (i) the agent's changing his mind about doing $X$ due to a change in circumstances, and (ii) the agent's being prevented from trying to do $X$ due to outside circumstances. Another qualification which they do not mention is also important here. The agent may change his mind about doing $X$ even if the circumstances of the situation are not believed to have changed and no new factors are believed to have been introduced. For the agent may change his mind about doing $X$ as a result of again deliberating about and re-evaluating exactly the same factors and circumstances as were involved in his previous deliberations. As a result of his further deliberation about these factors, the agent may come to believe that the proper thing for him to do is $Y$ instead of $X$. And he may thereupon decide to do $Y$ instead of $X$. Thus, on this view, for the agent to do $X$ is for the agent to believe that he will try to do $X$ unless he changes his mind about doing $X$ either because the factors are believed to have changed or because the factors have been re-evaluated or unless he is prevented by outside circumstances from trying to do $X$.

S. Hampshire and H. L. A. Hart, 'Decision, Intention, and Certainty', *Mind*, LXVII (1958), p. 11.

Another piece of evidence which tends to show that Hampshire and Hart hold the view being attributed to them is that they say, in discussing the topic of deciding: 'The certainty comes at the moment of decision, and indeed constitutes the decision . . .' when this certainty is arrived at in a certain way.[1] Their use of the term 'certainty' here strongly suggests that they believe that to intend to do $X$ is to believe very strongly that one will try to do $X$ (with certain qualifications).

Hampshire and Hart claim that if the agent admits that there is a possibility that a change in circumstances will lead him to change his mind about doing $X$, then 'there is at least a suggestion that . . . he does not yet really intend to do the future action'.[2] This does not seem to be correct. Let us suppose that the agent intends to do $X$ at $t_i$ because he believes that $C$ will obtain at $t_i$. His intention to do $X$ at $t_4$ is non-conditional with respect to every relevant circumstance. He may be as fully committed to doing $X$ at $t_i$ as it is possible for an agent to be when he has that sort of reason for intending to do $X$ at $t_i$, and yet he may admit that there are circumstances in which he might change his mind about doing $X$ at $t_i$. He might say that he is certain that $C$ will obtain at $t_i$ – this is why he is fully committed to doing $X$ at $t_i$ – and yet admit that it is possible that $C$ not obtain at $t_i$; and he might also say that if it were the case that $C$ did not obtain at $t_i$, he would change his mind about doing $X$ at $t_i$. The situation in which there is a suggestion that the agent does not 'really' intend to do $X$ is one in which the agent indicates that he believes that his previous deliberations will probably not be his final deliberations. This indicates that he has made a 'tentative' decision to do $X$. He has decided to do $X$ if he must do $X$ now or without deliberating about it further. But he has not completed his deliberations about doing $X$ and therefore has not made a final decision about doing $X$.

It is clear that not every strong belief by the agent that he will try to do $X$ (with certain qualifications) can count as an intention to do $X$. As Hampshire and Hart say, if the agent comes to have this belief on the basis of evidence – for example, on the grounds that in every situation like the situation in question, the agent has always done $X$ – this would not be the agent's having the intention of doing $X$. It is only when the agent comes to have the required belief on the basis of deliberation or on no basis at all that the agent's belief is an intention

[1] Hampshire and Hart, p. 3.
[2] Hampshire and Hart, p. 11.

to do $X$. (Hampshire and Hart do say that an agent can have a certain intention without that intention being the result of deliberation.)

The first objection to the Hampshire–Hart view has already been given in Chapter 5. It is this. The statement 'I believe that I will try to do $X$...' means 'I believe that I will do some action $Y$ and that my intention in doing $Y$ will be to do $X$.' For, as we saw in Chapter 5, trying to do $X$ consists in doing some other action $Y$ with a certain intention. But intending is being explained, by the view being considered, in terms of trying. And trying *is* explained in terms of intending. Thus, this view is not a satisfactory theory of intention, because it involves a vicious circularity.

The second objection to the Hampshire–Hart view is this. To have an intention to do $X$ is, on this view, to have a certain sort of belief, namely the belief expressed by 'I will try to do $X$ unless I change my mind about doing $X$ or am prevented from trying to do $X$ by outside circumstances.' But this explanation of what it is to have an intention is circular in another way. For it involves essential mention of the possibility of the agent's changing his mind about doing $X$. And since the agent's changing his mind about doing $X$ is a way of his ceasing to intend to do $X$, one does not know what it is for the agent to change his mind about doing $X$ unless he already knows what it is for the agent to intend to do $X$. But even if this is not circular, this attempted explanation involves an infinite regress. The belief which allegedly constitutes the intention is 'I will try to do $X$ unless I cease to intend to do $X$...', if we substitute the name ('ceasing to intend to do $X$') of the genus to which the process called 'changing one's mind about doing $X$' belongs for the name of this latter process in the 'unless' clause. But then the belief itself is partly about intending to do $X$. So we must replace the phrase 'unless I cease to intend to do $X$...' by its equivalent. The belief then becomes 'I will try to do $X$ unless I cease to believe that (I will try to do $X$ unless I change my mind about doing $X$...).' Further substitution gives 'I will try to do $X$ unless I cease to believe that (I will try to do $X$ unless I cease to intend to do $X$...).' This process leads to an infinite regress. On this view, then, the agent must have a belief that has an infinite number of clauses in its description. Hence this belief cannot be described. Therefore, this view does not explain what it is for the agent to intend to do $X$.

The third objection to this position is as follows. On this view the agent can come to have an intention to do $X$ by coming to have a certain belief on the basis of deliberation – that is, by deciding to do $X$. He can also come to have this intention by merely coming to have this belief on no basis at all. This makes it appear that the intention is identical with the belief. But if the agent comes to have this belief on the basis of evidence, he does not have the intention in question. Hence the intention is not identical with the belief. Instead, it is identical with such a belief, not when the belief is obtained in a certain way but rather when it is not obtained in a certain way, namely on the basis of evidence. But why is such a belief obtained by the use of evidence not an intention? Presumably it is because the basis of the belief in some way affects the nature or type of belief that the resulting belief is. But there do not seem to be different types of beliefs all of which have the same proposition as their object. When the agent believes on the basis of evidence that he will try to do $X$, he has exactly the same belief as he has when he believes that he will try to do $X$ as a result of having decided to do $X$. Of course, the two beliefs can have different strengths, but they are still the same belief. This theory of intention will not be satisfactory until it is explained how the fact that a belief of the sort in question has a certain basis can prevent that belief from being an intention. It is not the fact that the belief has a basis that prevents it from being an intention; for beliefs that are based on deliberation can be intentions. Nor is it even necessary for such a belief to have a basis in order that it be an intention; for, as Hampshire and Hart admit, some intentions have no basis, at least of the sort provided by deliberation. Thus, it must be explained why a belief's being based on evidence prevents that belief from being an intention.

Now let us turn to another view on what intentions are.

## 2. *Intentions, Beliefs, and Wants*

In Chapter 6 it was shown that intentions are in some respects very similar to final wants$_2$. I wish to discuss here a view related to this one, namely that in all cases, to have an intention is to have a certain group of beliefs and wants or one of a set of groups of beliefs and wants. I will try to show that this view is incorrect regardless of what types of beliefs and wants and what types of relations between them are mentioned by such a theory.

First, it seems that two people can have exactly the same beliefs and wants and yet one intend to perform a certain action while the other not intend to perform that action. Let us suppose that two men, Smith and Jones, both want $K$, and furthermore, want $K$ to the same degree. They also have the same beliefs about action $X$ and about the relation between $X$ and $K$, namely they believe that there is some chance but not very much chance that doing $X$ will bring it about that $K$ and that $X$ is the only possible way of obtaining $K$ if it is possible to obtain $K$ at all. It is certainly possible that in such a case, Smith decides to do $X$ and therefore intends to do $X$, while Jones does not decide to do $X$ and does not intend to do $X$. Smith explains his intending to do $X$ by saying that there is some chance that doing $X$ will bring it about that $K$. Jones explains his not deciding to do $X$ by saying that there is very little chance that doing $X$ will bring it about that $K$. Furthermore, each man agrees with what the other says. Smith agrees that the probability that doing $X$ will bring it about that $K$ is very low, and Jones agrees that there is some chance, though very little chance, that doing $X$ will bring it about that $K$. But Smith decides that it is worth a try while Jones decides that it is not worth a try. Thus, intending to do $X$ cannot be identical with having a certain set of beliefs and wants, for both men have the same set of beliefs and wants and yet only one of them intends to do $X$.

It will be replied that (i) these two men have different beliefs about the degree of probability that doing $X$ leads to $K$, or (ii) although both men desire the presence of $K$, they desire the presence of $K$ to different degrees – in particular, Smith desires the presence of $K$ more strongly than does Jones. But there are ways of determining whether they do have these different beliefs and whether their wants are of the same strength independently of whether or not they intend to do $X$. For example, that Smith and Jones each agree with what the other says about the probability of the doing of $X$ bringing it about that $K$ tends to show that they do have the same beliefs about this. Second, when asked about $K$, Smith and Jones may express equally strongly the desire for $K$ and, if told that $K$ is in fact present for both of them, may manifest joy and behave in other ways to exactly the same extent. And this would strongly support the claim that Smith and Jones desire the presence of $K$ to the same degree. If it is then said that the fact that Smith does intend to do $X$ while Jones does not intend to do $X$ nevertheless by itself shows that either they have different beliefs about the relation between $X$ and $K$ or that their desires for $K$ have different strengths, then the theory that to have an intention is to have a group of beliefs and wants is taken to be true by stipulation. For if this is said, then what an agent intends is taken as the criterion of his having beliefs and wants of the required sort.

## 3. *Intending to do X Because Doing X is a Duty*

Second, an agent can intend to do $X$ even if he does not want to do $X$ or even wants not to do $X$. For example, the agent may intend to do $X$ because he believes that doing $X$ is his duty. Therefore, to intend to do $X$ is not identical with having a certain set of beliefs and wants.

It will be replied that when the agent intends to do $X$ because he believes that doing $X$ is his duty, he does want to do $X$. For he wants to do his duty. And because he wants to do his duty and believes that doing $X$ is his duty, he wants to do $X$. So, even in this case, the agent wants to do $X$.

However, this objection is not sound. First, those who would claim that the agent in this case still intends to do $X$ out of desire must also hold that there are ways to determine what the agent desires other than by what he does or tries to do. For an agent can want to do $X$ and yet not do $X$. Some of these other ways of determining what the agent wants involve what the agent says. For example, if he says that he wants to do $X$ and expresses pleasure at the prospect of doing $X$, this serves as good evidence for the proposition that he wants to do $X$. Other such ways involve determining what the agent's behaviour is in various situations. For example, if he behaves in what we would call a 'joyous manner' upon being told that he can do $X$, this also serves as good evidence for the proposition that he wants to do $X$. And there are similar ways of determining that the agent does not want to do $X$ or even wants not to do $X$. For example, the agent may exhibit displeasure at the prospect of doing $X$. And it sometimes happens that the agent exhibits the manifestations which would be ordinarily taken to show that he wants not to do $X$ and at the same time does $X$ while giving as his reason for doing $X$ that doing $X$ is his duty. The most plausible description of such a case is that the agent did $X$ out of duty or because he believed doing $X$ to be his duty and not because he wanted to do $X$.

It may be replied that what these manifestations show is that the agent wants not to do $X$, so to speak, 'in itself'. They show that he does not want to do $X$ when $X$ is considered apart from its character of being the agent's duty. Nevertheless the agent does want to do whatever is his duty. For example, he would exhibit the manifestations which show that he wanted to do his duty upon finding out that action $Y$, which he performed without believing that doing $Y$ was his duty, was in fact his duty. And this agent does believe that doing $X$ is his duty. When such an agent does $X$, he does $X$ out of a desire to do his duty. Thus, in this case too, the agent has the intention which he has because he has a certain want – namely, to do whatever is his duty – and a certain belief – namely, that doing $X$ is his duty. Therefore, this case does not show that to intend to do $X$ is not identical with having a group of beliefs and wants.

But it is not true that if the agent indicates that he wants to do whatever is his duty and also indicates that he does not want to do $X$, but nevertheless does $X$ out of duty, he did $X$ because he wanted to do $X$. On the theory which we are considering, it is not sufficient that the agent wants to do whatever is his duty. He must also want to do that which he intends to do. For the theory holds that to intend to do $X$ is partly to want to do $X$. And in the case which we are considering, the agent intends to do $X$. So it must be shown that the agent not only wants to do whatever is his duty but also that he wants to do $X$. It must be shown that because he wants to do whatever is his duty, he wants to do $X$. But it is possible for the following to be the case: The agent indicates, by various manifestations before the question of his doing $X$ arises, that he wants to do whatever is his duty; he also indicates in a similar way, before he comes to believe that doing $X$ is his duty, that he wants not to do $X$; then, after he comes to believe that doing $X$ is his duty, he again indicates in similar ways that he does not want to do $X$. He then does $X$. This would show that the agent's desire not to do $X$ was stronger than his desire to do whatever is his duty. For even after he came to believe that doing $X$ is his duty, he still exhibited the manifestations which show that he wants not to do $X$. It is plausible to say that the agent wants not to do $X$ 'in itself' if he exhibits various manifestations of wanting not to do $X$ *before* he comes to believe that doing $X$ is his duty. But it is *not* plausible to say that this is still what is being shown when he exhibits these same manifestations *after* he comes to believe that doing $X$ is his duty. Then what must be said is that his desire not to do $X$ is stronger than his desire to do his duty. And thus his doing of $X$ cannot be explained by citing a desire. In such a case, his doing of $X$ can be explained only by saying that he did $X$ out of duty, in spite of wanting not to do $X$. Thus, before he did $X$, he intended to do $X$ and had this intention because he has a certain attitude towards duty. That he intended to do $X$ cannot be attributed to his having a desire to do $X$.

If it is still said that nevertheless the agent wanted to do $X$, then it is being denied that various sorts of manifestations can show that the agent wanted or wanted not to do $X$. But these sorts of manifestations do show this because we can determine that an agent wants or wants not to do $X$ even if he never does $X$. Hence the agent's intention in this case is not identical with his desiring to do $X$ together with his having various beliefs.

It might also be said that this theory need not hold that to intend to do $X$ is partly to have a desire to do $X$. This theory can hold that to intend to do $X$ is partly to have a desire which is related in some way to doing $X$, even if it is not a desire to do $X$. And the agent does have such a desire in the case being discussed since he does want to do his duty and believes that doing $X$ is his duty. His desire to do whatever is his duty is related to doing $X$ because he believes doing $X$ to be his duty.

But at most this theory could hold only that having a desire which is related to doing $X$ and not necessarily a desire to do $X$ is a necessary condition of intending to do $X$, not that it is also a sufficient condition (along with having certain beliefs) of intending to do $X$. For there could be a case in which the agent does want to do whatever will bring it about that $K$, wants not to do whatever will bring it about that $L$, believes that doing $X$ will bring it about that both $K$ and $L$, and does not intend to do $X$. Here the agent has two desires which are relevant to doing $X$ and yet does not intend to do $X$.

Thus, to intend to do $X$ is not identical with having a set of beliefs and wants.

# 10  Intentions as dispositions

## 1. *Introduction*

The dispositional element in mental states has recently been emphasized by philosophers. In this chapter I will consider whether a dispositional analysis can be given of intentions.

The version of what we might call the Dispositional Theory of
Intention which I will discuss is as follows: the statement

(I) I intend to do $X$ at $t_4$

is identical with

(II) If the situation now had been in all relevant respects just like
the situation which I expect to prevail at $t_4$, I would have done
$X$ now.

It might be suggested that a simpler dispositional translation of (I)
would be something like 'If the situation at $t_4$ were to be as I now
expect, then I would do $X$ at $t_4$.' Both this simpler version and (II)
refer to both the present and the future. They *must* do so, for (I) is
*about* both the present and the future: *I now* intend to do $X$ at $t_4$.' The
difficulty with the simpler version is that it only asserts that expectation
is present at the time of the statement, while (II) says that more than
this is present. (II) says that the agent is now in a certain state of
readiness to perform $X$, not just that he has certain expectations concerning the situation at $t_4$. For this reason, (II) seems to me to come
closer to expressing what (I) asserts.

First, I will further explain this theory. Then I will present several
serious objections to it.

## 2. *What the Dispositional Theory of Intention Claims*

On the Dispositional Theory of Intention, statements of intention
such as (I) have the import of counterfactual conditionals. For this

theory – or at least this version of this theory – claims that statements such as (I) are identical with statements such as (II). Statements whose meanings are explained in terms of conditional statements are said to be 'dispositional statements'. Thus, statements of intention are dispositional statements. They are dispositional statements which are partly about the moment at which they are made and partly about a future moment $(t_4)$, as (II) is. They are not at all predictions about what the agent would or will do at $t_4$, not even conditional predictions as we saw in Chapter 8. When an agent expresses his intention, he is not predicting that he will do $X$ at $t_4$. He is talking about what is or might have been the case at the moment at which he makes his statement of intention and is doing so partly by referring to what he expects to be the case at $t_4$.

It is because a statement of intention is about the moment at which it is made that the agent can later change his mind about doing $X$ after making that statement without that statement thereby being shown to be false. However, it is true that on this dispositional view, the agent cannot intend at $t_1$ to do $X$ at $t_4$ (non-conditionally) while believing that the situation at $t_1$ is exactly like the expected situation at $t_4$ in all relevant respects and yet not have done, tried to do, or be trying to do $X$ at $t_1$. If the agent does not do $X$ at $t_1$ in such a case, either he must believe that $t_4$ is in some respect a better time or a more appropriate time to do $X$ than is $t_1$ and that therefore $t_1$ and $t_4$ are in fact not the same in all relevant respects – in which case he can still intend at $t_1$ to do $X$ at $t_4$ since statement (II) can still be true even if $t_1$ and $t_4$ are not alike in these ways – or else he does not intend at $t_1$ to do $X$ at $t_4$. It is usually acknowledged that the agent cannot intend at $t_4$ to do $X$ at $t_4$, believe that the moment in question is in fact $t_4$ and that the expected situation prevails, and yet not be doing or trying to do $X$ at that moment. And this is just the limiting case of the requirement just stated, where the moment at which the agent has the intention is identical with the moment at which he intends to do $X$.

In saying that statements of intention are about the moments at which they are made, I am construing the term 'now' as a token-reflexive term. That is, (II) is taken to be identical with

(III) If the situation at the moment at which this statement is being made had been in all relevant respects just like the situation expected at $t_4$, I would have done $X$ at that moment.

We cannot replace the term 'now' in statement (II) by names of moments such as '$t_1$', '$t_2$', and so on. For an agent may not know the name of the moment at which he makes his statement of intention and yet he can certainly express his intention at that moment. Moreover, in stating his intention, he typically does not use any expression which is the name of the moment at which he states his intention.

It might be objected, however, that (I) ('I now intend to do $X$ at $t_4$') and (III) cannot be identical for the following reason. Let us suppose that statement (III) is made after time $t_4$. Statement (III) would be meaningful if made then, but statement (I) would not be meaningful if made after $t_4$. Hence statements (I) and (III) cannot be identical. But it is not true that statement (I) cannot be meaningful if made after $t_4$. As we saw in Chapter 3, if the agent believes that it is possible for him to affect the past – for example, if he believes that time travel into the past is possible – then his statement that he intends to do $X$ at $t_4$ might very well be true and would therefore certainly be meaningful. If statement (I) would be meaningful on some such occasion, it would, like (III), be meaningful on all such occasions; when the agent did not have such beliefs about the past, statement (I) would be false but still meaningful. And this supports the position that (I) and (III) are identical. For this position also holds that (I) would be meaningful on all such occasions because it holds that (I) is identical with a statement, namely (III), which is meaningful on all such occasions.

It might also be objected that if (I) is identical with (III), then it is not possible for an agent to express the same intention at two different times. For on the view being discussed, when he expresses his intention to do $X$ at $t_4$, he refers to the present moment; and hence on each such occasion, he refers to a different moment. Since on each such occasion the agent is talking about something different, namely a different moment, the agent cannot be saying the same thing and hence cannot be expressing the same intention. However, there is a difference between talking about the same thing and saying the same things. After all, the statement 'The President of the United States is tall' made in 1861 and the statement 'The President of the United States is tall' made in 1966 are the same statement, in one sense of the term 'same statement', even though each is about a different person. And the agent makes the same statement, in at least this sense of the term 'same statement', when he expresses his intention at two different times by uttering the sentence 'I intend to do $X$ at $t_4$.' Moreover, on each such occasion he is talking about most of the same things that he is talking about on the other occasion, namely himself, an action, and the moment $t_4$.

## 3. Statements of Intention as About Both Present and Future

Statements of intention are not only about the future. They are about among other things, the moments at which they are made. In many cases, a statement of intention will mention a future time explicitly; and, as we will see, in those cases in which a future time is not explicitly mentioned, a future time could have been mentioned. But on the view being discussed, when the future time is mentioned, it is mentioned only to identify or refer to a certain situation – a situation which is expected to be present at that future time. By saying that he intends to do $X$ at $t_4$, the agent indicates that he expects the circumstances on which his performance of $X$ depends to be present at $t_4$. But he is nevertheless saying what he would have done *now* or *at the time at which he states his intention*. He is not predicting what he will do at $t_4$, as we saw in Chapter 8. So far it has been said that the meanings of statements of intention are to be rendered by conditional statements such as (II). But they can perhaps be better rendered in the following way. In making statement (II)

> (II) If the situation now had been in all relevant respects just like the situation which I expect to prevail at $t_4$, I would have done $X$ now.

the agent would not only be making a conditional statement but he would also be making a non-conditional or categorical statement. By saying that if a certain situation which he expects to be present at $t_4$ were or had been present now, he would have done $X$ now, he says in part that he expects a certain situation to be present at $t_4$. The statement 'I expect a certain situation to be present at $t_4$', which is one of the things that he says in making statement (II), is a categorical statement. Thus, statement (II), and hence statement (I) 'I intend to do $X$ at $t_4$', are identical with

> (IV) I now expect that a certain situation will be present at $t_4$, and if that situation had been present now, I would have done $X$ now.

Statement (IV) is not a purely conditional statement; it is partly conditional and partly categorical – that is, it is a conjunction of a conditional statement and a categorical statement. Such statements are called 'semi-hypothetical statements'. Thus, on this view, statements of non-conditional intentions are semi-hypothetical statements.

On this theory, the reason why statements of intention seem to be about the future is that they *are in part* about the future. They are, in part, expressions of belief about future times. But these beliefs concern *circumstances and situations* at those future times. They do not concern *the performance of actions* at those future times. So while it is true that statements of intention are in part about the future, these statements are not about the future in the way in which predictions of future *actions* are about the future. Thus, this view can show both in what way statements of intention are about the future and why these statements are not necessarily false if the agent does not perform the actions in question at those future times.

### 4. *Inseparability of Actions and the Agent's Being Disposed to do X*

Now I wish to raise two serious objections to the Dispositional Theory of Intention. These will be put forward and discussed in this section and in Section 5.

The statement 'I now intend to do $X$ at $t_4$' is said by the Dispositional Theory of Intention to be synonymous with the semi-hypothetical statement 'I now believe that a certain situation will be present at $t_4$ and if that situation had been present now, I would have done $X$ now'. But it might be objected that this latter semi-hypothetical statement could be true and yet the statement 'I intend to do $X$ at $t_4$' not be true. For it is possible that the only intentions which the agent has are the intention to do $Y$ at $t_4$ and the intention to do $Y$ whenever situation $S$ is present. And yet the above semi-hypothetical statement concerning $X$ could still be true. Let us suppose that in a given situation doing $Y$ is inseparable from doing $X$ – that is, that in this situation the agent cannot do $Y$ without doing $X$. And let us also suppose that the agent does not know or believe that doing $Y$ is inseparable from doing $X$. The agent expects situation $S$ to occur at $t_4$ and has the non-conditional intention to do $Y$ at $t_4$ because he expects $S$ to be present at $t_4$. So the agent satisfies the categorical conjunct of the above semi-hypothetical statement because he has this belief about the presence of $S$ at $t_4$. It is also true that if situation $S$ had occurred at $t_1$, the agent would have done $Y$ at $t_1$, since he has the intention to do $Y$ whenever situation $S$ is present. But it follows from this that he would have done $X$ at $t_1$ also, if situation $S$ had been present at $t_1$. For he would have done $Y$ at $t_1$ if $S$ had been present at $t_1$, and by hypothesis an agent cannot do $Y$ in this situation without also doing $X$. Therefore, the conditional conjunct of the above semi-hypothetical statement, namely 'If that situation (the situation expected at $t_4$, in this case $S$) had been present now, I would have done $X$ now', is true (if we take 'now' as used here to refer to $t_1$). Thus, if (i) the agent intends now (at $t_1$) to do $Y$ at $t_4$ because he believes that situation $S$ will be present at $t_4$, (ii) the agent intends to do $Y$ whenever $S$ is present, (iii) if the agent does $Y$ at $t_1$, he will also do $X$ at $t_1$, and (iv) the agent does not know or believe that if he does $Y$ at $t_1$, he will do $X$ at $t_1$ and may even believe that (iii) is false – if all of these are the case, then the above semi-hypothetical statement will be true. That is a situation in which the semi-hypothetical statement concerning $X$ is true even though the agent does not intend at $t_1$ to do $X$ at $t_4$. Thus, the statement 'I intend to do $X$ at $t_4$' cannot be identical with this semi-hypothetical statement. For there is a situation in which the latter is true while the former is false.

It might be replied that if the agent were to do $Y$ at $t_1$ because he believed that $S$ was present at $t_1$ and hence also does $X$ at $t_1$, the agent would be doing $X$ unintentionally at $t_1$. For the agent would be doing $X$ at $t_1$ without knowing that he is doing so, since he is intentionally doing $Y$ and does not know or believe that doing $Y$ is inseparable from doing $X$. In order to rule out this type of case, we therefore need only add the term 'knowingly' to the consequent of the conditional conjunct of the semi-hypothetical statement concerning $X$: 'If that situation had been the case at $t_1$, I would *knowingly* have done $X$ at $t_1$.' If the agent does do $X$ knowingly – in particular, if he does $Y$ voluntarily and knowingly, as is the case in the above example, and at the same time knows that he is doing $X$, perhaps because he knows that doing $Y$ is inseparable from doing $X$ – then the agent does $X$ intentionally at $t_1$. For he is then doing $X$ knowingly and voluntarily at $t_1$. And hence the semi-hypothetical statement would not be true in the situation characterized by (i), (ii), (iii), and (iv). For the conditional conjunct of that semi-hypothetical statement, when the term 'knowingly' is added, is true only in a situation in which the agent would have done $X$ intentionally, whereas in the situation characterized by those four conditions, the agent would have done $X$ unintentionally at $t_1$.

However, if we add the term 'knowingly', then on the modified position the agent can intend at $t_1$ to do $X$ at $t_4$ only if it is the case that if the agent were to believe that $S$ is present at $t_1$ and were to do $X$ at $t_1$ because he had this belief, he would do $X$ *intentionally* at $t_1$. That is, his doing $X$ knowingly at $t_1$ in such a case would be a necessary condition of his intending at $t_1$ to do $X$ at $t_4$. But the former is in fact not a necessary condition of the latter. For he can intend at $t_1$ to do $X$ at $t_4$ and yet do $X$ at $t_1$ unintentionally if he comes to believe that $S$ is present at $t_1$. This would be the case if he did intend at $t_1$ to do $X$ at $t_4$ and at the same time conditions (i)–(iv) were satisfied. If conditions (i)–(iv) were satisfied, then the agent would do $X$ unintentionally at $t_1$ if he came to have this belief about the presence of $S$ at $t_1$. And it is certainly possible for the agent to intend at $t_1$ to do $X$ at $t_4$ at the same time that conditions (i)–(iv) are satisfied. Therefore, it is possible that the agent intends at $t_1$ to do $X$ at $t_4$ and yet would do $X$ unintentionally at $t_1$ if he came to have the belief in question. So we cannot add the term 'knowingly' to the consequent of the conditional conjunct of the semi-hypothetical statement. For if we did so, there could be a situation in which the modified conditional conjunct, and hence the complete semi-hypothetical statement, is false and yet the agent's statement 'I intend to do $X$ at $t_4$ (made at $t_1$) is true.

Thus, if we do not add the term 'knowingly' to the conditional conjunct, there is a possible situation in which the conditional conjunct and the categorical conjunct, and hence the semi-hypothetical statement, are true and yet the statement 'I intend to do $X$ at $t_4$' (made at $t_1$) is false, namely the situation in which conditions (i)–(iv) are satisfied and yet the agent does not intend at $t_1$ to do $X$ at $t_4$. But if we do add the term 'knowingly' to the conditional conjunct, then there is a possible situation in which this conditional conjunct is false and hence the complete semi-hypothetical statement is false and yet the statement 'I intend to do $X$ at $t_4$' (made at $t_1$) is true; this situation is that in which conditions (i)–(iv) are satisfied so that the agent would do $X$ unintentionally at $t_1$, thus rendering the conditional conjunct false, and yet the agent does intend at $t_1$ to do $X$ at $t_4$. Thus, in either case the statement 'I intend to do $X$ at $t_4$' (made at $t_1$) and the semi-hypothetical statement about $X$ have different truth-values and cannot be identical with one another.

## 5. Deciding and Dispositions

A second objection to the version of the Dispositional Theory of Intention previously presented is this. It may be true that an agent expects a certain situation $S$ to be present at $t_1$, and it may also be true that if the agent were to come to believe that $S$ were now present, he would also do $X$ now; and yet it may be simultaneously true that the agent does not now intend to do $X$ at $t_4$. For example, the agent may expect $S$ to be present at $t_4$ and yet not have decided what he will do at $t_4$ in that situation. It was claimed in Chapter 4 that to decide to do $X$ at $t_4$ is to come to have the intention to do $X$ at $t_4$ after a process of deliberation which has certain characteristics. If so, then since the agent in this situation may still be undecided about what to do in the situation which he expects to prevail at $t_4$, it is possible for an agent in this situation not to do $X$ at $t_4$ yet. For example, the President of the United States may now expect the countries of Europe to lower their tariffs on non-European goods in 1972 by fifty per cent; and it may also be true that if he came to believe that they had done so today instead of in 1972, he would order United States tariffs reduced today by the same percentage. That is, he would in fact decide to order such a reduction and would carry out this decision. Yet he may rightly deny that he now intends to lower tariffs by fifty per cent in 1972; he may say that he has not yet decided what to do in that situation. So the requirements of the Dispositional Theory are met in this case and yet the agent does not have the intention in question.

One who holds the Dispositional Theory of Intention might reply that this objection can be answered by adding a categorical conjunct to such statements as (VI) and (VII) of the following form: 'and the agent believes that conjunct $\Phi$ is true', where the expression 'conjunct $\Phi$' refers to the conditional conjunct of (VI) or (VII), depending on whether it is (VI) or (VII) that this statement of belief is being added to. For it might be claimed that the agent cannot expect that $S$ will be present at $t_4$, be disposed to do $X$ now if he came to believe that $S$ were now present, *believe that he is so disposed*, and yet not intend to do $X$ at $t_4$.

But the agent could have this belief solely on the basis of evidence. That is, he could believe solely on the basis of evidence that he was so disposed. And since he can have such a belief on the basis of evidence without intending to do $X$ at $t_4$, adding this belief to his belief about $S$

being present at $t_4$ and his being disposed to do $X$ now if he comes to believe that $S$ is present will not render it any more necessary that he intend to do $X$ at $t_4$ than it was before this belief was added. An agent could expect $S$ to be present at $t_4$ and correctly believe that he is disposed to do $X$ now if he comes to believe that $S$ is now present, without intending to do $X$ at $t_4$. For this latter belief could be based solely on evidence. It is true that in order to use what he did in past situations as evidence of his dispositions with regard to the present situation, the agent must know what factors exist in the present situation so as to be able to determine what past situations are sufficiently similar to the present situation and can therefore be used as evidence about the present situation. But the agent could know what factors exist in the present situation and yet not have deliberated about them together with $S$. Thus, he may not yet have decided what to do in a situation like the present one in which $S$ is also present. Hence he may still not intend to do $X$ in such a situation. And in particular he may still not intend to do $X$ at $t_4$ when he expects such a situation to be present.

# Conclusion

Now it is time for a very brief summary of what I have tried to do in this book. I have been trying to find out something about what intentions are. In Part Three several general theories of intention were examined and found inadequate. These theories were found inadequate because they seem to admit of counter-examples or to involve vicious circularities or regresses. But I hope that the discussion of these theories together with what was said in Parts One and Two serves to show us some of the characteristics for which such a theory must account in order to be adequate.

One of the outstanding characteristics to be accounted for is the way in which an intention seems to have one foot in the present and the other foot in the future. I tried to bring this out in comparing statements of intention with predictions. Of course, this is not unique to intentions. But more must be determined about the precise relations that intentions have to the present and the future. Is a present intention to perform a future action related to present and future in just the same way in which a belief which one now has about a future event related to present and future? Is a statement of intention *about* present and future in just the way in which a statement of the form 'It is now probable that $E$ will occur at $t_i$' is about both present and future? And even if the answer to each of these questions is 'yes', what exactly are these relations? We must find out more about these relations. And once this has been done, a general theory of intention must explain what intentions are in such a way as to allow intentions to have these relations.

In Part One intentions were divided into the categories 'purposive' and 'non-purposive'. If I am right in claiming that intentions do divide into these two categories and in describing the differences between them, then a theory of intention must account for these differences. Purposive and non-purposive intentions differ markedly in important ways. For example, the former is a type about which the agent can change his mind while the latter is not. So a general theory of

129

intention must show how two things which differ so greatly in important ways are nevertheless two varieties of the same thing.

Most of Chapter 2 was spent in establishing that there is an important difference between conditional and non-conditional intentions. I made a suggestion about what the basic difference between them might be, but in my opinion everything still remains to be done on this point. And again, whatever the basic difference between them turns out to be, a general theory must take this into account; it must at least allow intentions to differ from one another in this way.

Chapter 3 put forward a number of theses about objects of intention. For example, a person can intend to do $X$ only if he does not believe that doing $X$ is logically impossible. Why are beliefs and intentions related in this way? And in what other ways are they related?

Other facts about intentions were developed in Part Two. In addition, Part Two outlined the close relations between intending on the one hand and other states and activities such as choosing, deciding, and trying on the other. This helps to show that with an adequate theory of intention we will have taken a large step towards a theory of the mind.

# Bibliography

Note: This bibliography lists some of the books and articles which deal (wholly or in part) with intention, with closely-related activities such as deciding, choosing, trying, and deliberating, and with philosophical problems in which the notion of intention figures. This bibliography makes no claim to being complete, and is intended only to indicate the range of topics and problems in this area given attention in the literature.

ANSCOMBE, G. E. M., *Intention*, Basil Blackwell, Oxford, 1957.
ARDAL, P., 'Motives, Intentions, and Responsibility', *Philosophical Quarterly*, XV (1965), pp. 146–54.
ARISTOTLE, *Nicomachean Ethics*, Book III, Chapters 1–5.
AUNE, BRUCE, 'Intention', in Paul Edwards (ed.), *Encyclopedia of Philosophy*, Macmillan–Free Press, 1967, Volume Four, pp. 198–201.
——, 'Intention and Foresight', *Journal of Philosophy*, LXIII (1966), pp. 652–4.
AUSTIN, JOHN, *Lectures on Jurisprudence*, John Murray, London, 1873, Volume I, pp. 433–7, 449–54; reprinted in Herbert Morris (ed.), *Freedom and Responsibility*, Stanford University Press, Palo Alto, California, 1961.
BARNES, W. H. F., W. D. FALK, and A. DUNCAN-JONES, 'Intention, Motive, and Responsibility', *Aristotelian Society Supplementary Volume 19* (1945), pp. 230–88.
BECK, LEWIS WHITE,' Conscious and Unconscious Motives', *Mind*, LXXV (1966), pp. 155–79.
BEDFORD, ERROL, 'Intention and Law', *Journal of Philosophy*, LXIII (1966), pp. 654–6.
BENTHAM, JEREMY, *An Introduction to the Principles of Morals and*

*Legislation*, Basil Blackwell, Oxford, 1948, pp. 200–21; reprinted in Morris, *op. cit.*

BROADIE, FREDERICK, 'Trying and Doing', *Proceedings of the Aristotelian Society*, LXVI (1965–6), pp. 27–40.

CANFIELD, JOHN, 'Knowing about Future Decisions', *Analysis*, XXII (1962), pp. 127–9.

COX, J. W. R., 'Can I Know Beforehand What I am Going to Decide?' *Philosophical Review*, LXII (1963), pp. 88–92.

D'ARCY, ERIC, *Human Acts*, Oxford University Press, Oxford, 1963.

DAVENEY, T. F., 'Choosing', *Mind*, LXXIII (1964), pp. 515–26.

——, 'Intentions and Causes', *Analysis*, XXVII (1966), pp. 23–8.

EDWARDS, REM B., 'Is Choice Determined by the Strongest Motive?' *American Philosophical Quarterly*, IV (1967), pp. 72–8.

EVANS, J. L., 'Choice', *Philosophical Quarterly*, V (1955), pp. 303–15.

FLEMING, BRICE NOEL, 'On Intention', *Philosophical Review*, LXXIII (1964), pp. 301–20.

GALLAGHER, K. T., 'On Choosing to Choose', *Mind*, LXXIII (1964), pp. 480–95.

GAUTHIER, DAVID P., 'How Decisions Are Caused', *Journal of Philosophy*, LXIV (1967), pp. 147–51.

——, 'How Decisions Are Caused (But Not Predicted)', *Journal of Philosophy*, LXV (1968), pp. 170–1.

GINET, CARL, 'Can the Will Be Caused?' *Philosophical Review*, LXXI (1962), pp. 49–55.

GLASGOW, W. D., 'On Choosing', *Analysis*, XVII (1956), pp. 135–9.

——, 'The Concept of Choosing', *Analysis*, XX (1959–60), pp. 63–7.

GUSTAFSON, DONALD, 'Momentary Intentions', *Mind*, LXXVII (1968), pp. 1–13.

HAMPSHIRE, STUART, 'On Referring and Intending', *Philosophical Review*, LXV (1956), pp. 1–13.

——, 'Reply to Walsh on Thought and Action', *Journal of Philosophy*, LX (1963), pp. 410–24.

——, *Thought and Action*, Chatto and Windus, London, 1960.

HART, H. L. A., and STUART HAMPSHIRE, 'Decision, Intention, and Certainty', *Mind*, LXVII (1958), pp. 1–12.

HANCOCK, ROGER, 'Choosing As Doing', *Mind*, LXXVII (1968), pp. 575–6.

HEATH, PETER, and JOHN PASSMORE, 'Intentions', *Aristotelian Society Supplementary Volume 29* (1955), pp. 131–64.

JENKINS, JOHN J., 'Motive and Intention', *Philosophical Quarterly*, XV (1965), pp. 155–64.

KAUFMAN, ARNOLD, 'Ability', *Journal of Philosophy*, LX (1963), pp. 537–51.

——, 'Practical Decision', *Mind*, LXXV (1966), pp. 25–44.

KENNY, ANTHONY, *Action, Emotion, and Will*, Routledge and Kegan Paul, London, 1963.

——, 'Intention and Purpose', *Journal of Philosophy*, LXIII (1966), pp. 642–51.

KOLNAI, A., 'Deliberation Is of Ends', *Proceedings of the Aristotelian Society*, LXII (1961–2), pp. 195–218.

LEHRER, KEITH, 'Decisions and Causes', *Philosophical Review*, LXXII (1963), pp. 224–7.

LONG, THOMAS A., 'Hampshire on Animals and Intentions', *Mind*, LXXII (1963), pp. 414–16.

MACINTYRE, A. C., *The Unconscious*, Routledge and Kegan Paul, London, 1958.

MELDEN, A. I., *Free Action*, Routledge and Kegan Paul, London, 1961.

NOWELL-SMITH, P. H., 'Choosing, Deciding, and Doing', *Analysis*, XVIII (1958), pp. 639.

O'CONNER, JOHN, 'How Decisions Are Predicted', *Journal of Philosophy*, LXIV (1967), pp. 147–51.

RANKIN, K. W., *Choice and Chance*, Basil Blackwell, Oxford, 1961.

RYLE, GILBERT, *The Concept of Mind*, Hutchinson, London, 1949.

SAMEK, R. A., 'The Concepts of Act and Intention and their Treatment in Jurisprudence', *Australasian Journal of Philosophy*, XLI (1963), pp. 198–216.

SELLARS, WILFRID, 'Imperatives, Intentions, and the Logic of 'Ought', in H-N Castaneda and G. Nakhnikian (eds.), *Morality and the Language of Conduct*, Wayne State University Press, Detroit, Michigan, 1963.

SHWAYDER, DAVID, *The Stratification of Behavior*, Routledge and Kegan Paul, London, 1965.

STOCKER, MICHAEL, 'How to Prevent Self-Prediction', *Journal of Philosophy*, LXV (1968), pp. 475–7.

TAYLOR, RICHARD, *Action and Purpose*, Prentice-Hall, Englewood-Cliffs, New Jersey, 1966.

——, 'Deliberation and Foreknowledge', *American Philosophical Quarterly*, I (1964), pp. 73–80.

THALBERG, IRVING, 'Intending the Impossible', *Australasian Journal of Philosophy*, XL (1962), pp. 49–56.

WALSH, JAMES J., 'Remarks on *Thought and Action*', *Journal of Philosophy*, LX (1963), pp. 410–24.

WHEATLEY, JON, 'Hampshire on Human Freedom', *Philosophical Quarterly*, XII (1962), pp. 248–60.

WHITE, ALAN R., *The Philosophy of Mind*, Random House, New York, 1967.

WILLIAMS, GLANVILLE, *Criminal Law: The General Part*, Stevens and Sons, London, 1953, pp. 28–45, 77–81; reprinted in Herbert Morris, *op. cit.*

ZINK, SIDNEY, *The Concepts of Ethics*, St Martin's Press, New York, 1962.

# Index